"Does Spelling Count?"

"Does Spelling Count?"

Written by a teacher for *everyone* because
everyone *was* a student
at one time or another.

Nancy Y. Fillip

Copyright © 2010 by Nancy Y. Fillip.

ISBN: Softcover   978-1-4535-6163-8

All rights reserved. No part of this book may be reproduced or transmitted in any form or by any means, electronic or mechanical, including photocopying, recording, or by any information storage and retrieval system, without permission in writing from the copyright owner.

All names in the book have been changed for privavcy reasons. Any name that is the same is entirely coincidental.

This book was printed in the United States of America.

To order additional copies of this book, contact:
Xlibris Corporation
1-888-795-4274
www.Xlibris.com
Orders@Xlibris.com
85797

CONTENTS

Preface		9
Chapter One	How It All Began	13
Chapter Two	A Calling	23
Chapter Three	Making a Difference	31
Chapter Four	Say That Again?	37
Chapter Five	Other Points of View	41
Chapter Six	How Long is Your Fuse?	51
Chapter Seven	You Have to Laugh	57
Chapter Eight	Taking Risks But Never Cheat	66
Chapter Nine	You Mean I'm Not Fired?	74
Chapter Ten	Teacher Anxiety	83
Chapter Eleven	Role Reversal	87
Chapter Twelve	Connections	96
Chapter Thirteen	Drama Queen	101
Chapter Fourteen	Final Stories	107
Chapter Fifteen	Closure	112

ACKNOWLEDGEMENTS

Of course I couldn't have written this book without the support of a slew of people. But before I get into the specifics, it really all began back in college with a wonderful freshman biology professor of mine who convinced me that I was intelligent. Up until that day, I didn't believe in myself. So, thank you professor for lighting my candle and planting the seed that could fulfill my dreams someday. Prophetically, he was being a model of the type of teacher I have become today. My friend Krishnabai was the one who put the idea in my head when she said to me one day, "I wonder if there is a book in you?" At the time I told her, I doubt it." Now here I am. So thank you Krishnabai for the impetus to get things cracking. And for the support along the way.

Many thanks and hugs to my family for their support and contributions. They always stand behind me. They are my rock. Thanks to my sister Elizabeth Young for proofing and full support. To Megan Beaudette for proofing and lending a good ear as I read countless chapters for her positive feedback. I am indebted to James Davis who edited, proofread and patiently showed me what and what not to do as a writer. Being a "newbie" I had so much to learn. His critiquing helped to shape my book and create the exact manuscript I was looking for. Many thanks to James for his time and effort. I am thankful for Christyanne Rothmel who also spent some time with me with sound advice. Thank you to Beulah Grenough, Caroline Rumsey, and Erin Gentile for their hours of proofing and poring over the manuscript fine tuning my book.

And last, to my contributors, thank you for your honesty, candidness, and participation that rounded out my book. Monica Bacon, Nicole Beauchesne, Linda Casceino, Jeannie Erikson, Adrienne Fillip, Carla Fillip, Vanessa Fillip, Lydia Kowalski, Margaret Meyers, Noelle Nanto, Sara O'Leary, Kyle Sparkane, and Cynthia, David, Emily, Lindsey, and Nikki. Thank you to all my students who fueled my passion for living.

PREFACE

I'm a teacher. There are more than six million of us in the country, all of whom probably have a book in them. So why would you want to read my book? It's different. That's why. This isn't a book on how to become a better teacher. Nor is it a book on quality curricula or how to raise your standardized test scores. I'm writing from my heart about what happened in my classrooms over the past 34 years. You will discover my philosophy about teaching from a humorous and poignant point of view. Now that I have retired, reflections on my experiences give me tremendous pleasure. My mind is like a storage bin full of memories. Joy, passion, patience, frustration, and annoyances are all blessings teaching can offer. Whether you are a teacher, parent, or student, it is my hope you'll connect with my thoughts.

I love teaching and believe I was given a gift to be an educator. I never felt like I was going to "work." Often times it felt like a calling. (That might have had something to do with the salary!) Never once have I regretted my choice to become a teacher. My secret fantasy in life was to become a medical doctor. But obviously that didn't happen. So I chose plan B. Be a science teacher. The hours of teaching in the lab, doing dissections, and keeping up with new frontiers of science satisfied my desire to attend medical school. I wouldn't go back and do anything different.

Changes in education regarding curriculum, methodology, pedagogy, and philosophy have created numerous twists and turns since I began teaching. These often presented challenging moments. Kids today live in a different world from when I began my career. Major socio-economic changes have created a different kind of student since 1976.

Yet, the more things change, the more they stay the same. What do I mean? When I was in school in the 60s and 70s, drugs were prevalent. The youth of that time were pressured to engage in psychedelic drugs to counteract the current culture. We have a drug problem today. According to the National Survey of Household Drug Abuse, 6.7% of those people twelve years and older use illegal drugs every month. I had peers in my class whose family members were fighting in Vietnam. Today we deal with students whose family members are serving our country in Iraq or Afghanistan. Economically, the 70s were marked by an energy crisis. There was the realization oil reserves were not endless. Today we have an energy efficiency crisis and struggle with the rising costs of oil. Colleges are still competitive and it's not just because of academics. Students still have the burden of outrageous tuitions. And kids still get homework and have to be in school on time. Incidentally, Massachusetts was the first state to enact a compulsory attendance act back in 1852. It required all children (except those living in poverty, disabled or deemed knowledgeable) to attend school for at least three months between the ages of eight and fourteen. At least six weeks had to be consecutive. Failure to comply with these requirements? A fine of $20.00.

In the end, kids are still kids no matter what year it is. They still learn, laugh, cry, spar with their peers and forget to bring their pens to class. Kids are still asking, "Mrs. Fillip, does spelling count?" These students will continue to boost our self-esteem and drive us crazy. Frequently we wonder what inner drive would cause us to subject ourselves to dealing with dozens of kids every day.

Does Spelling Count is a book for everyone whether you teach or not. At one time or another, we've all been students. If you're not a teacher, I hope you'll laugh at the anecdotes, be inspired with my philosophy, resonate with my experiences, or just be entertained. If you're a parent, then don't read this until your kids graduate. Just kidding!

Enjoy!

I REMEMBER WHEN...

Too many kids would say on test day, "The test is **today**?"

Sandy told me she did not have her homework done because she was unconscious all night.

Drew told me he could not eat milk products because he was lactating.

The kids saw me in my pajamas at Nature's Classroom and Jon said that he never knew that teachers actually wore pajamas. (I don't know *what* he thought we wore to bed)

Jimmy said his mission in life was to introduce kangaroos all over Australia.

Shawna turned to me after receiving her communion wafer during mass and said, "Got milk?"

CHAPTER ONE

How It All Began

"Teaching should be such that what is offered is perceived as a valuable gift and not as a hard duty."—Albert Einstein

It's game time and already things are going wrong. The alarm went off at 6:00. I roll over and promptly shut it off. I *though*t I hit the snooze button. Forty-five minutes later I'm startled awake, something is just not right. The lighting outside seems different. I glance over and see the clock reads 6:45. Yikes! I have fifteen minutes to wash up, get dressed, grab some breakfast, and leap into my car. "Okay, I tell myself. I can do this." Just as I'm about to leave, the second snafu of the morning rears its ugly head. The car keys are missing. "Anybody seen the keys to the van?" I yell. No response, of course. Everyone else is running around getting ready themselves. The keys are eventually located under a stack of unopened mail. Phew!

Now in the car, I encounter the day's third snafu. Halfway to school I realize I forgot the three boxes of baking soda needed for today's lab. Shoot! There is no way to do this lab without that stuff. I decide to stop at a mini-mart to pick some up. Snafu number four! While rummaging around in my pocketbook for some cash, I notice my glasses are missing. Groan! They're sitting on my nightstand. "That's just great," I think. I can't get through the day without my glasses. As if on auto pilot, the van glides into the parking lot. I dash into the minimart. They only have one box of baking soda. Of course. That's why it's called a "mini" mart. It's not a *super*market. What was I expecting? Okay. One box is not going to work for me. Back in the car. Instantly my mind starts thinking up Plan C. I don't *have* a Plan C. Meanwhile, what am I going to do without my glasses for the day? Ho Hum. I'm beginning to think it might have been a good day to stay home in bed. When I arrive at school, I'm already physically and mentally exhausted. I walk through the doors and I am assaulted with shouts of "Hey, Mrs. Fillip. How ya doin?" They don't want to know how I am *really* doing. Feeling frazzled, I put on my game face, smile, and cheerfully reply, "Hey guys. I'm just fine."

- I'm a teacher. You're a teacher. Every day we teach somebody or ourselves something. Anybody can be a teacher. The difference is, can you inspire? Ho Boon Tiong, the Principal Consultant of Classpoint Consulting, an educational training and consulting firm, once said, "The more you prepare outside of class, the less you perspire in class. The less you perspire in class, the more you inspire the class."

When I'm home, the tasks of being a parent seem so daunting. Managing a household and children can be overwhelming. When I'm in school, I am given more kids and issues to deal with than any parent will ever have. Suddenly, my own children's problems seem minimal. The students in my class are not my kids. They come from many different backgrounds and cultures. They have a variety of learning styles. Some are mature and others never seem to grow up. They have varying states of emotion. There are days I wonder if they are learning anything at all or if they're just being shuffled through the system. Mainly, I learn to cope with and handle a plethora of situations in hopes of reaching positive outcomes. If a student doesn't do his or her homework, or doesn't behave in class, I can't take away their computer privileges at home. Constantly I feel the need for inspiration.

On the matter of teaching, I am passionate about what I do. Throughout the past 34 years, I have been a teacher in the classroom, a coach on the field and in the gym, and tutor of instrumentals. Nothing gives me greater pleasure than seeing a student make connections, enjoy their learning, and continue on to be successful. On the flip side, nothing bothers me more than seeing a student fail. Like a parent of my own children, it's easy to blame myself and wonder why I didn't do more. When I began teaching, my initial goal was to ensure *every* child in the classroom was successful. When that didn't happen, I took it personally. Over the years I realized I couldn't make students learn. But I did come to realize it was my responsibility to educate, motivate, and inspire. It has been said that schools are a place of detention for children placed in the care of teachers who are afraid of the principal, principals who are afraid of the school board, school boards who are afraid of the parents, parents who are afraid of the children and children who are afraid of nobody.

There is some truth to that. When I was a child, pupils were afraid of their teacher or the principal. There was a different level of respect. Being sent to the principal's office was scary. Many of my students welcome the chance to be removed from class for a spell. The idea of being disciplined by administrators does not carry the same weight. As an adult *I still* fear the principal. Imagine this: I am in the middle of teaching, and the principal pops her head in my door. "Nancy, can you see me at the end of the day in my office," she asks. Immediately I think, "Oh no, what I have done wrong this time?" That's it! I turn into a dishrag. My brain immediately starts racing through my mental catalog to remember any intervention with a student or parent which might have upset someone. It takes a monumental effort to teach for the rest of the day. I can barely concentrate. Forget about lunch! Finally, at 2:30 I slowly walk to the principal's office awaiting my doom. I begin to think, "What could I do in life if I get fired? Teaching is all I do and love." The principal is pleasant, smiles and asks me to sit down. She begins with the proverbial statement, "The reason I called you in here today is because . . ." I hold my breath. She asks, "Do you think you could put together a dance for the students in grades 6-8?" I am so relieved this is *all* she wants that I say yes a little too quickly. As the adrenaline drains out of my body and I begin to come back to my normal state, I feel like I would have climbed Mt. Everest for her. Phew! Of course I don't mind giving up my Friday night to be at a dance for 150 crazy, sweaty, chaotic, middle-scho**ol**-age kids**.** I mean**,** I have just spent an entire week with them. Why not Friday night as well? Because of my own fears, I'm sensitive to a student's emotions when I ask him or her to see me at the end of the class. I let them know they've done nothing wrong. Otherwise, that child will not be on board with me for the rest of class. Instead they'll be wondering what they might have done wrong. Letting a student hang is just cruel. I know. I have been there.

* * *

Nothing burns me up more than having someone tell me being a teacher is the easiest job in the world. Obviously they've never been a teacher. They exclaim, "You have free evenings, and you get weekends, school vacations and a whole summer off." Yes I do. But those are the times to regain my sanity. However, during those "free times" I don't stop being a teacher. The preparation work for teachers is never ending. A typical school day begins early in the morning, *before* the students arrive. Based on how ambitious I am feeling, I prepare for the day logistically and mentally. I might need to male copies. The copying machine *always* has a line of at least four teachers; especially when I'm in a hurry. It's at those times I beat myself up wondering why I didn't make 200 copies of a worksheet on the parts of a cell *before* I went home yesterday. Interestingly, the Xerox method of copying by using light, an electric charge, and dry powder is called xerography. It was developed and patented by a physicist named Chester F. Carlson. The word xerography is a Greek word meaning "dry writing." In Rochester, New York, the Haloid Company bought the patent. They changed the name to Xerox and made an empire of Carlson's process. I remember when we used to make copies on the mimeograph machine. Purple paper, purple ink and purple hands everywhere. When Xerox came out with the copy machine, it was such a welcome relief—until we were limited to 1000 copies a month. Trying to decide what should be on paper and what shouldn't became the game of the day. If I ran out of copies before the month was up, I could stand around waiting for another unsuspecting teacher to use the machine. Discreetly I would try to see their paper count and tactfully think up a way to ask if I could "borrow" some copies.

Days can be grueling. My teaching demands I wear several different hats. Trying to find out why Scott has not done his homework forces me to be a psychologist. Students constantly asking for Band-aids or cough drops makes me a nurse. Writing lab reports requires attention to detail so I become the enforcer. Then Amber and Janey (who are best friends) are not talking to each other and my role is mediator. Crash! Off the lab table rolls a test tube. Another job is to find the broom and become the custodian. At 3:00, when the students depart, I get to sit back, kick my feet up, and wonder where the nearest chocolate stash is. Unless of course I have a faculty meeting, department meeting, a parent conference, need to engage in extra help for students, or run an extracurricular activity. Why is it when the kids finally go home, my desire to consume anything less than 500 calories a bite is exponentially magnified? I'll go on a mission looking for anything slightly resembling simplified sugars. If I'm lucky, snacks will be served at a faculty meeting. I dive in as though I have been put on a starvation diet for the past three months. Does teaching really make me hungry? Or am I so stressed out at the end of the day I need a quick fix?

As I mentioned, school doesn't stop when the kids go home. The monumental task of correcting stacks of school papers or preparing lessons for the next day awaits me. The warm afternoon sun beckons me. Suddenly I can't wait to get out of the classroom. I start negotiating in my head which part of the day is going to be sacrificed doing schoolwork: the afternoon or the evening? Or do I wait until the weekend? How many countless Sunday afternoons have I spent sitting on the couch with mounds of papers knowing I promised to get them back to the students on Monday. I don't need to wonder why I waited all weekend to correct them.

I glance across the room and see 75 projects sitting on the lab tables. "Hmmm, when am I going to correct those? Fantasies start erupting in my brain. I'm thinking of devious ways to correct them quickly. Perhaps if the student meets all the requirements of the project they will get an A. Then grade from there. But my conscience gets the better of me. I know the students have put long, hard hours into their projects. They deserve my time and fair assessment. Oh wait, I have another idea. Maybe I can correct them over the school vacation. It's easy to get trapped into thinking I have the *entire* vacation to correct papers and projects. Then I realize I am not having a vacation after all. So I wait until the last day of vacation, pull a grading marathon, and hit the sack well after midnight. I drag myself into school Monday morning exhausted and blurry eyed from so much correcting. Smiling, of course.

* * *

Have you heard of the school bag syndrome? At the close of school each day, I pile up all the papers I am going to take home and correct. Ha! Once I arrive home, free of kids who need me all at once, I am greeted by my *own* children who need me all at once. My good intentions of sitting down with that school bag gets further and further from reality. After shuffling my own children to their extracurricular activities, make dinner, clean up dinner, and help my kids with their homework, maybe, just maybe, I'll have time to drag out the school bag. Is that what I really want to do now? Start correcting papers at 9:00? In reality, all I want is a hot shower, or some down time with the TV. I love to read but usually I'm so tired I end up falling asleep with the book on my face. I rationalize that the papers can wait another night. The school bag goes to school with me the next day—full of uncorrected papers. I ask myself over and over, "Why do I bring this bag home every night?

* * *

What else does a teacher do besides teach all day, correct papers, and make lesson plans? Teachers must attend meetings for IEP students. (Individualized Educational Plan). These are plans for students who need special accommodations while in the classroom to ensure successful outcomes. There are faculty meetings, team meetings, meetings for your department, and professional days. I am assaulted with forms which seem to come out from every crack in the building that need to be filled out and returned "yesterday." There are scheduled and spontaneous parent conferences. And nightly phone calls to parents about Jason not doing his homework that need to be documented. There is extra help before school, during my lunch break (if I'm willing) and after school. We have important conversations behind closed doors with other teachers. For example, why is it that Mario is always signing out for the bathroom in every class (He is probably trying to hook up with Melissa who is signing out for the girl's room) and what can we do about it? Most schools would prefer you undertake an extracurricular activity as I guess they assume we are *not* busy enough with our jobs. Some of the programs can keep you at school until well after 5:00 and sometimes later. The whole time you are responsible for kids. Responsible, all the time!

* * *

Do you remember when you were learning to drive? The day I got my license (40 years ago) I was very excited to take the car out by myself. My parents told me I could take a trip to the grocery store to buy some cat food. I flew down the driveway, leaped into the car, started her up and began to back out. Of course I did the all the right things by looking left, then right, then left one more time to make sure no one was coming. What I forgot to do was to look directly behind me! I stepped on the gas pedal and zoomed out into the street. Crash! I smashed right into a car parked next to the sidewalk. With shock and dismay on their faces, my parents were watching me from the living room window. My father came running out while I stood in the street, totally embarrassed but scared about what was to come next. I turned to my father and immediately said, "Sorry. But it's a good thing we live in Massachusetts, because we have no-fault-insurance which means we won't have to pay for it because it's nobody's fault, right?" I could hear my mother yelling in the background, "That's it. No driving for a month."

As a parent of four teenage drivers, I've probably thought the same thing myself. Even innocent accidents are costly and a hassle; not to mention the insurance rates going up. But it's a catch-22. If I ban them from driving, how do I let them get the experience to be a better driver? Sitting in the house and thinking about "what they've done" is not going to improve their driving skills. Teaching is the same way. It parallels learning to drive. I can go to college, take courses on instruction, and learn about curriculum and methodology. But the only way I can become a better teacher is to actually teach. Nothing replaces the experience of being in the classroom. Someone told me if you can survive through the first three years, most likely you'll be a teacher forever.

Undeniably, the first couple of years featured a huge learning curve for me. I was prepared to make many mistakes. No one expects you to be perfect. After a few years I became comfortable with my curriculum. I started to understand what makes kids tick. The strategies used to teach and control behavior started to fall into place. I become cognizant of what works and what doesn't work. Suddenly my focus was less on methodology. Knowing and enjoying my students became the number one priority. Then it hit me. I love teaching and was meant to do this. It didn't take long for me to realize I was given a gift to teach. Going to work every day was not a job. The thrill of being in the classroom gave me energy, purpose, and a higher sense of self-esteem. While the salaries were always on the low side, that was secondary. I knew I was doing what I love, five days a week. How many people wake up in the morning and say they love their job? Some of you may say yes but so often I hear people complaining how they hate their job.

In the past 34 years I moved around from school to school. For several years I taught at U-32 Junior-Senior High School in Vermont. The kids, the curriculum, and the beauty of the land made this job idyllic. It was an interesting school being the first in the state of Vermont to have an open classroom.

What is an open classroom? An open classroom is a student-centered classroom design that was popular in the United States in the 1970s. In the school where I taught, it was constructed without inner walls, which made teaching loud and disruptive. This was a problem as well as proper ventilation and maintenance. In other open classroom schools, the design inside the building allowed a large group of students of varying skill levels to be in a single, large classroom with several teachers overseeing them.

This was derived from the one-room schoolhouse, but sometimes expanded to include more than two hundred students in a single multi-age and multi-grade classroom. In my school we were in individual "areas" with no walls to separate the kids. It is an adjustment the first month for students and teachers. Particulary for the incoming seventh graders and new faculty. In addition, all staff, including administrators are on a first name basis for students which was disconcerting to me. I was raised traditionally and the idea of students calling me Nancy instead of Mrs. Fillip took getting used to. After students have learned how to minimize disruption to their fellow students (which I believed they never really learned), the real work of the school year begins. When I went to college in Vermont, I was told repeatedly *not* to do my student teaching at U-32 High School because it was an open classroom school. So I didn't. I taught in Williamstown. When I graduated from college I moved to New York for a few years and then got married. My husband is an environmental engineer and when he finished his masters, jobs for environmental engineers in 1978 were limited. He had two offers—Nashville, Tennessee or Montpelier, Vermont. Unless he wanted a quickie divorce, we were definitely headed back to Vermont.

Guess where I eventually got a teaching job? U-32 Junior-Senior High School. Though I loved working there, I would be remiss to say it wasn't a challenge. The concepts of no walls presented themselves with some interesting problems. Classes were lined up one after another with nothing in between save an occasional bookcase. This allowed students to peer into other classrooms and have conversations with one another. (There was no texting then.) The crescendo of noise became intolerable because there was nothing to absorb the sound. At least twice a day a teacher would put two fingers in her mouth and give off an ear-splitting whistle. The noise of the students would instantly cease and you could actually hear a sigh of relief. Slowly the noise would start to build again until it was time for the whistle. Because I taught science, I had the luxury of sharing a lab which *had* walls. It was a welcome relief a few times a day not having to police student's behavior due to wall-less situations.

When I moved to Massachusetts, I couldn't find a high school position and landed a job teaching middle school. I fell in love with those kids. Although my experience working with high school children was tremendous, middle school kids were not the "monsters" everyone had me believing. It was there in middle school I felt I had found my stride as a teacher. My middle school teaching years involved a Catholic school, a charter school, and a public school. Every place I worked housed wonderful students, supportive administration, friendly co-workers, and a mission to provide the best learning opportunities possible. This book is a compilation of experiences from the schools where I taught. Included are some vignettes from my coaching years as well. While you're reading, perhaps you can relate to the stories and situations I found myself in over the past 34 years. Some stories are poignant, many hilarious, and others revealing as to why I became a teacher. I hope they strike a chord with anyone who reads them regardless of whether you're a teacher, parent, or student. No matter what year it is, or where I teach, kids continue to learn, and touch my life. This is unequivocally universal. Teaching is what you put in and what you get back. With some effort, teaching becomes a two-way street and you reap the benefits of this amazing relationship.

I REMEMBER WHEN...

Lizzy asked me in class why islands don't float away.

Larry asked me what day Super Bowl Sunday was on.

Gail asked me if SPAM was the plural of Spray PAM.

Kyle asked me if text books had words in them.

Brian told me he couldn't hear me because
he had his eyes closed

Todd told me he was not chewing gum. It was sugarless wax.

CHAPTER TWO

A Calling

One looks back with appreciation to the brilliant teachers, but with gratitude to those who touched our human feelings. The curriculum is so much necessary raw material, but warmth is the vital element for the growing plant and for the soul of the child. ~Carl Jung

Why do I teach?

When I think about my life as a teacher, I am reminded of the public education trailblazer, Horace Mann. He retired from his law practice in 1837 to become Massachusetts' first Secretary of Education. Ironically, from ages ten to twenty, he only attended school six weeks of the year. He educated himself by reading extensively from the public library. Seeing public school as a way to improve and equalize educational opportunity, Mann comprehensively surveyed the condition of the state's schools, established training institutes for teachers, increased the length of the school year to six months, and gathered support for more funding for teacher salaries, books and school construction. I am grateful for his crusade as being educated is a privilege and being a teacher is an honor.

Originally it seemed I wasn't destined to be a classroom teacher. When I married, I moved to Vermont where no teaching jobs were available. As a result, I landed a job working in a book store. I didn't feel so bad. After all, when Einstein graduated from The Swiss Polytechnic University he went to work in a patent office. This actually turned out to be ideal for him because it gave him time to work on his physics. During that time he wrote five papers on various theories which earned him his doctorate.

It changed the way the world understands physics. Which in turn led to a teaching job.

I never wrote any brilliant papers at the bookstore, but I quit after four months and actively sought out a teaching position. My efforts resulted in a job teaching Physical Education. I worked in a Junior-Senior High School in Vermont with my first experience teaching a completely outdoor physical education program. If it wasn't raining, we were outside. Some of our curriculum included lacrosse, ice skating, and biking. I was never in better shape than the times I was teaching Phys. Ed. Interestingly, my coworker at the time had built a dynamic ropes course at the school. Rope courses are amazing engineering feats that engage students in climbing. Using such a course, students can participate in a variety of challenging and empowering activities. Students were outside every day and actually enjoyed gym class. Getting kids to dress appropriately will forever be a problem for P.E. teachers. Here we were in the middle of winter in Vermont. The kids were whining because I demanded they wear a hat for class. Girls were particularly difficult as apparently "hat hair" is not acceptable for the remainder of their school day. Another issue was hygiene. When the students came back to the locker room after gym class, they were expected to take a shower. I am sure there are many grown adults today who talk about the ways they tried to skirt around the required shower. As a teacher, I walked a fine line in demanding students take those darn showers. I was caught between watching them *take* a shower and not trying to come across as a pervert. I knew if they returned to their next period class smelling like old, sweaty socks, I was in trouble. I know many girls did the "shower without actually going under" the shower. This involves sticking the lower part of all your limbs in the water while wearing a wrapped towel. It gives the illusion of taking a shower. I most likely did the same thing in junior high.

* * *

Each day, an eighth grader named Danielle came into the class, sat down, and prepared herself for the day. As she lifted up her desk cover, she found a magazine ad for Rogaine inside. Rogaine is used to treat male baldness. She was clueless as to who put it there or why. This happened for about five days in a row. On the fifth day she came in, opened up her desk and there was the ad for Rogaine, again!! "That's it, she yelled. I've had it. Who keeps putting this ad for Rogaine in my desk? I don't need to lose any weight."

If you have ever experienced working with middle school-age students, you know every day is different. Every day is diverse and interesting but you better be prepared to expect the unexpected. I love that! This is one of the reasons I have spent half my teaching career working with this age group. While my morning starts with a frustrated Danielle, nobody prepares you for this kind of a problem. It reminds me of parenting. Where's the manual for unusual situations? I try to track down who is cutting out ads for Rogaine, while taking attendance, preparing for teaching and wondering if Danielle is still upset. This is a typical example of a teacher playing many roles. The Rogaine mystery forces me to be a super sleuth and psychologist while doing my teacher duties. Ten minutes later Danielle is fine and laughing with her friends. That's adolescence. That's teaching in a middle school classroom. You may be familiar with the tough times adolescents experience. Their body is in confusion, physically changing and developing. Emotionally they are on a roller coaster. You're never sure what or who is going to upset them. It's difficult at times to get answers out of them. If you are a teacher and/or a parent you know the drill: Hannah is looking like she just lost her best friend. "Is something bothering you, Hannah?" you ask with sincere concern. The response might be an emphatic "no" as they put their head down on the desk or walk sullenly to their room and slam the bedroom door. Hmm. Obviously *something* is bothering her. These youngsters are trying to become independent thinkers and problem solvers. Because they are teenagers, I used to tell the parents of my students: "They have a teddy bear in one hand and a beer in the other." During countless conferences I hear parents tell me they don't know what happened to their perky, polite, sixth grader from last year. I tell the parents this is not atypical and soon their child will become human again. The changes going through their bodies physically and emotionally are dramatic for them. At times they themselves don't even understand why they feel the way they do.

Social interactions are an integral part of an adolescent's life. One of the ingredients to make a good middle school teacher is to understand and be compassionate toward students and their relationships with their peers. Part of the job of teaching middle school is providing insight to the students about "getting along." I tell my kids you can't pick your boss and you can't pick your coworkers. Life is all about getting along with each other and working cooperatively. As a science teacher, I work in the lab frequently. Because of limited equipment, I have students work with a partner. Each month I would change their partners by drawing names out of a hat. I swear the kids got more nervous over this monthly drawing then they did for a test. There was always varying amounts of body language displayed around the room as the two names were called. I saw looks of delight and dismay as the names were matched up. When I was teaching seventh and eighth grade, I noticed many of the girls were decidedly interested in the boys. By eighth grade the interest in the opposite sex was more evenly matched. Grouping students together for labs and projects becomes a chance for social interaction. There is an increase of hand holding under desks, flirting, and note passing between students.

One afternoon I was outside doing recess duty. Scanning the area I noticed there was a small group of eighth graders huddled in a circle next to the wall of the building. One student kept turning around and looking out as though they were the "scout" for the group. Instinct told me *something* was going on. (Maybe some of you know what I mean. It's that same feeling you get when your toddler is in the other room and suddenly it's *too* quiet.) I wandered over to the group and immediately a few students took off. No way were they going to be an accessory to a crime. As I peered into the circle I saw Emma and Peter locked mouth to mouth. They didn't even notice I was standing there. Apparently the circular posse was protecting their indiscretions. As I verbally pried them apart, they were not the least bit ashamed. I didn't know the protocol, as I had never encountered French kissing on the playground. Where was the manual for that? Part of me hated to turn them in, but I knew in a matter of minutes the gossip grapevine would have the story all over the school. If my principal found out I had washed my hands of the incident, my head would be on the chopping block. I had no recourse but to take them to the main office. As I explained to my boss what happened, I could see her trying not to turn up the corners of her mouth. "Send them in," she said. I envisioned the two students having to stay after school and writing 500 times, "I will not French kiss." However, detentions were assigned, parents informed, and that was the last time there was any French kissing on the playground.

How have students changed since I started teaching?

Probably one of the biggest changes I have seen in the past 30 years is the level of respect for the teachers from the students. When I was in school, answering back to a teacher in a rude or disrespectful manner earned you a trip to the principal's office. You always spoke to the teacher using his or her name. "Yes, Mrs. Rose." "No, Mrs. Clark." "Thank you, Mr. Campbell."

While I still demanded the same level of respect, students today are quite bold. If I am teaching and I see Melissa chatting with her friend, I will stop for a minute and ask Melissa to please stop talking. Her response is apt to be, "I wasn't even talking." Does she think I was imagining it? Use of expletives, lashing out with anger, and disruptive behavior seems more prevalent than many years ago. There is no question society has influenced how students behave today. Kids used to go home, step off the bus, and find a mother happily baking cookies in the kitchen. Today there is often a single parent who is probably not at home but working. We have a huge generation of latch key kids. What do they do when they get home? I hope they are plopping down at the kitchen table and whipping out their two hours of homework. But I know this doesn't happen. The television, video games, and the computer beckon these kids. Technology has become the surrogate parent. I can't tell you the number of parent conferences I have had with frustrated parents who tell me they "thought" their child was doing their homework every afternoon. Many parents will say, "But when I ask Willy if his homework is done, he either says he has done it, doesn't have any, or he did it in class." After 34 years, I can count on one hand the number of times I allowed my students to do their homework in class. Hence the name, *home*work.

How has education changed since 1976?

When I began my teaching career, the average student's desire to learn felt stronger. I don't remember having to be so motivational in my teaching techniques. Now I feel I have to be more creative, inspirational, and hyper vigilant about each individual student to allow them to be successful in my classroom. Part of the time teaching requires more classroom control and dealing with individual issues with particular students. Kids don't seem to react to the threat of being removed from the classroom because of poor behavior. Many of them are happy to leave. Having full control of my students is one of my strengths. For me, I think it was innate but it can be learned. My time spent at a military college and officer training school at McConnell Air Force Base gave me skills I used in the classroom as well. Students seem to sit up and fly straight when I come into the room. Learning to achieve the balance of being firm and still earning the respect from your students takes time. However, the first day sets the tone. I have seen too many teachers who are too "nice" in the beginning of the year and then try to regain the upper hand. That's the hard way to do it. I never had a problem speaking to a student who was misbehaving. If the misbehavior continued, I simply took the student out from the rest of the class. The purpose of the private conversation is to inform them their behavior is unacceptable. With concern, I ask what is making them act up in class. After a conversation that does not berate the student, I offer choices because defiance is often part of autonomy. The choices are: come back in the classroom and settle down or take a trip down to the principal's office. When students are given choices, most often they will choose to stay in the room. Ultimately, I don't want them out of my class. I never removed a child from my classroom unless they were deliberately keeping another student from learning. Every person in the room has the right to learn and not be disrupted by someone else.

We have more resources and access to more efficient, faster information than before. And yet, ironically, I believe kids today are not motivated and seem to take these advantages for granted. Technology is out there and there is a belief we have to use it. If a teacher is going to use computers in the classroom, they must have a plan in place to make sure the computers are being used solely for the lesson intended. I think too much time is wasted browsing on the Internet. Teachers have to police what sites students click on. Have you ever tried watching 30 computers at once? Kids are sneaky. They can be typing a paper and be on another site at the same time. Conversely, everything I know about computers came from my students. For example, they taught me about making PowerPoints, which I talk about later. When I first started using computers, nobody gave the "seasoned" teachers tutorials on how to use them effectively in our classrooms. I always felt like I was *forced* to learn things about the computer. I'll be honest when I say I did *not* embrace the computer age. Pac man was even too difficult for me. There was tremendous pressure to keep up with changing technology. As the new generation of students and teachers caught on, the older generation fought to accept it. Even when I *tried* to be competent on the computer, I swear my brain would not retain any of the knowledge. It has been frustrating and sometimes humiliating to constantly ask for help. Oh, give me my red grade book and a ball point pen any day.

Kids today are bombarded with a fast moving world. Culture requires them to keep up with the fast pace of computers, video game, cell phone, iPods, MP3s and all the other gadgets. I swear kids today are born with different brain cells allowing them to become experts on all the new-fangled stuff. Because of all the technology to entertain them, it seems students get bored easily in class. The shift from one activity to another need to move along with the same frenetic pace they find in the technology they use. Let's face it. Kids today are multi-taskers and electronic geniuses. They can be on the computer and talk on their cell phone at the same time. They text while watching television. I still can't get my head around my old Nokia phone. Daily I monitor the class for texters. Did my fifth grade teacher need to speak to me about texting during class? No, I probably was sent to the corner of the room for putting my feet on the chair in front of me.

I am aware computers are helpful and have mastered some skills that some of my own generation can't do, so I feel I have made progress. Once I mastered the PowerPoint there was no stopping me. Out with the overheads and in with new, colorful, and dynamic presentations. Some of you might remember the overhead. It brings back tortuous memories of high school history, sitting in the back of the auditorium (and I mean "back" as were seated alphabetically and my maiden name was Young) trying to stay awake while the teacher lectured us incessantly with his overhead projector. Yawn! As a teacher, I hated that piece of media equipment. First you had to "sign" it out. Why couldn't they have one for every class? With the overhead you needed *two* hands. One hand to write with and the other to make sure that stupid plastic transparency did not slide around. And even worse. Was it upside down? Now, with PowerPoints, a teacher can lean back and with the click of a remote in one hand and a coffee (or water) in the other, present an inspiring and engaging lesson. (I wonder if kids are sleeping in the back of *my* class?) By the way, once I had a student fall asleep in first period biology. I decided to leave him there until he woke up. He didn't wake up until third period! That was before PowerPoints!

I REMEMBER WHEN...

Tim sneezed in class and the force of his sneeze caused his head to slam down on the fire alarm button.

I had to break up a fight between Samuel and Joey because they were arguing over whom would look better wearing a dress.

Elizabeth tried to pierce her ear using my three-hole punch.

Jay insisted that Kentucky was the capital of Tennessee.

Kate was late to class because she told me she got her hand stuck in the paper towel dispenser.

Robert told me studying history was stupid because it already happened.

CHAPTER THREE

Making a Difference

The task of the excellent teacher is to stimulate "apparently ordinary" people to unusual effort. The tough problem is not in identifying winners: it is in making winners out of ordinary people.
~K. Patricia Crossa

It is a proven fact teachers can make a difference in a child's life. Their actions and your words can alter the path of a youngster. I also know from personal experience that negative thoughts from teachers can make a lasting impression. A teacher in my high school told me I was "too stupid" to go to college. Can you imagine that? Then he told me if I insisted on going to college, maybe I should consider a junior college and transfer. I thought my dad was going to blow a gasket. I ended up at Norwich University and made the Dean's List first semester. But the damage had been done in high school. For a long time I truly believed I wasn't smart enough to achieve whatever I wanted. When I think back on all the teachers and professors I ever had, the ones who made a difference in my life were not necessarily the ones from whom I earned the best grades. Those teachers gave me confidence and made me believe I could achieve whatever I wanted.

Secretly I hope my students will look back with fond memories and regale stories of how I was the best teacher they ever had. Without a doubt, I believe that will happen with some. Conversely, there are probably many students who hope they never catch sight of me again. I sincerely believe anyone who teaches grabs the spotlight at one time or another and has their moment to shine. We all make a difference in at least one child's life. Never in my teaching career did I allude to any student that they weren't capable of achieving. As a new teacher in 1976, my mission was to make sure every student truly learned. What a shock when I found out there were students who were apathetic about their education. "What? You don't care?" I use to worry that if every student wasn't doing well or eagerly soaking up the knowledge, I was failing as a teacher. I soon figured out not every child learns the same way, and children do not process everything I say. My educational training did not include a course on differentiated instruction. That buzz word did not come out until several years later. I think I was doing differentiated instruction right from day one but it never had a name. In the class, it was obvious all students cannot move at the same pace. While my philosophy was to teach to the higher end of the spectrum, the class was tailored to meet the needs of all my students.

Convincing children they can be successful at whatever they want does not preclude some of the more frustrating moments that call on my absolute patience. This includes students who are not listening in class when I give directions for an activity. After ten minutes of explaining today's lesson I tell them to get to work," Ten seconds later I hear the usual, "What are we supposed to do?" My first instinct is sarcasm. "What, were you out getting popcorn the last ten minutes?" But I patiently smile, ask what it is they don't understand and start all over again. The worst scenario involves a kid who is in the bathroom while I'm explaining some important instructions. He comes strolling back to class and nonchalantly asks, "What are we doing now?" If I had a dollar for every time I responded with exasperation, "*I just went over everything,*" I could have retired a long time ago.

* * *

If you have children, you might relate to this next scenario: Teaching your own children. Wait, is that an oxymoron? Can you *possibly* teach your own children? Working together to learn a new skill should be a partnership but here is a case in point. It's the year 1999. My daughter is ten years old. Being an accomplished pianist, I want her to learn to play the piano as well as I do. The introductory lesson goes well. I assign her music to practice until the next lesson. With any young child I teach, it is my expectation the parent will take an active part in their learning process. One day after the lesson, I remind my daughter she needs to practice. "*I know,*" she says. The day comes to a close and she has not practiced. On the second day I remind her she missed practicing yesterday and needs to hop up on the piano bench and begin. "I will after I . . ." After she talks on the phone, checks her email, watches two TV programs, takes a dip in the pool, plays with the dog, eats a bag of Doritos, or who knows what else? Now I start to lose my patience. I tell her I'm starting the timer for 30 minutes for practice and all her other extracurricular activities need to be put on hold. "Mom, I still have five days until the next lesson. What's the big deal?" she asks. I think to myself that the $20.00 I would shell out to Mrs. Rodham next door for lessons would be worth it. But then, the struggle would still follow as I play "Polly practice piano police officer." *All* my attempts at teaching my children something have not been futile. But it can be difficult because your own children, as opposed to those in the classroom, can take liberties on their behavior. I can take liberties regarding my degree of patience and tolerance for their behavior. Am I going to send them to the principal's office if they are sarcastic?

When I was teaching in a Catholic school, all my daughters attended the school. Initially they were not old enough to be in my class. The school was so small that each grade only had one teacher per grade starting from fifth grade. Over a period of nine years, I had my daughters in class for three years. If you can place your own child in a different class other than your own, then I'd recommend it. But that was not possible in this school. Each of my children responded differently to me being their teacher. I found an interesting article on teaching your own children in the classroom. "Having your own child in your classroom may not be a great idea. Parents tend to be harder on their children than others. While many outsiders will feel that you are giving your child favors and special attention, you will be trying so hard not to that you actually treat your child worse than the other students. In addition, children need space. They need to have friend arguments without their parents knowing it. They need to get called down in class once or twice without their parents knowing it. They need to make a couple of bad grades on a test and be given the chance to tell their parents without their parent knowing it first. I believe that the older the child is the harder it may be to have him or her in class and keep peace at home with the family. It would be just too hard not to bring up things that happen at school. Some schools will not allow a parent to have his or her own child in class if it can be prevented. Even if your school does allow it, it may not be a good idea. Think it over before attempting it. Consider how it might affect both your child and your job."

I certainly agree with many of those points. Conversely, having my children nearby all day kept me informed far more than if they were in a school where I wasn't teaching. The only exception was my son who did not attend school where I taught. He was extremely independent and I felt I didn't have to keep an eye on him as much. He was an excellent student and kept me informed. My daughters were younger and logistically this made it more difficult to have them attend school elsewhere. I wasn't comfortable having them come home after school without me being there. So they ended up at my school and I ended up being their teacher. I was probably harder on them than the other students. Not only did I worry that people might think I am allowing my kids to get away with things, my own children worried what their friends would think. If they earned a good grade on a test, some peers might suggest I showed them the test the day before. I never did that but there is no evidence to back that up. One of my daughters had some friends ask her to find the test at home so they could have the questions ahead of time.

I tried my best to treat my children like every other child. They called me Mrs. Fillip in class. Except for the time Adrienne screamed out, "Mom!" when she couldn't get my attention. I enjoyed having them in the class and sharing my feelings about certain situations regarding students or ideas for class. We had an understanding that whatever I said about the school that wasn't worth sharing, they would not give me away. My daughters honored that from day one. Because we had this trust, some of the conversations in the car on the way home from school were full of honesty, and laced with humor. For example, we could be candid and open about how a teacher handled the food fight in the cafeteria. I knew that whatever we said, it would not be repeated. I allowed my girls to be themselves at school and didn't pry into their social lives. The advantage was being there and having that peripheral vision. When another teacher would come and tell me about some indiscretion from one of the girls, I always stopped them first and asked them, "If I wasn't in the school, would you be calling home about this?" It became the benchmark for deciding whether another teacher could take advantage of having me in the school to solve the problem rather than the teacher dealing with it.

My children, for the most part, enjoyed having me as a teacher. After the first day of school, one of my daughters said she was initially embarrassed to have me as teacher. Eventually she settled in. And since she was not terribly motivated as a student, she never worried her friends would think she was profiting from her mother being the teacher. Vanessa, another daughter, told me I was too loud. I do have a loud voice. (And all my children are loud today. They did *not* inherit that from their father.)

On the first day of school I tell all my students I have a loud voice and not to mistake that for yelling. Never could my own kids tell me at home they have no homework because I assigned it! It was helpful in quizzing them for tests because I knew what direction the exam would be going. My daughter mentioned that she feels parents do too much for their kids today. While this was not a problem when I was her teacher, she recalls a few assignments when she thought she became exempt because I was her teacher. My youngest daughter thought having me in class was "cool." She felt I treated her fairly and said the kids in the room liked me as a teacher so there were never any issues.

Today, my daughters and I reminisce and laugh about our times together. When Adrienne was in eighth grade, I had a student from her class approach me and ask if he could take her out on a date. I told him he was more than welcome to walk her to the water fountain any day of the week. Vanessa reminded me of a humiliating episode where I took her aside and began to trim her bangs in front of the entire class. (I don't know *what* I was thinking!) When one of my girls bopped her classmate on top of the head with her pencil box, I took her in the hallway and read her the riot act. She came back in with a slip that had to be signed by her father. The rest of the class was astonished. "But your mother saw you do it. And you still have to bring a slip home?" her classmates exclaimed. Those moments established credibility for me as a fair teacher and helped show my daughter she was like everyone else.

Sometimes it's difficult having an outside job and leaving your children home or in the hands of a babysitter. Being a teacher to my kids eliminated the feeling I wasn't spending enough time with them. While I saw them every day in the classroom, there were special times when we would meet up in the hallway or library and I could just chat with them. I enjoyed that. If a crisis happened during school, I was there to comfort them. It's hard to convey to family members at home things that happen at your job. I could talk about my day and my children knew exactly what I meant. Having them in my classroom afforded me more advantages than having them in other schools.

I REMEMBER WHEN...

I was choking on a piece of a granola bar and the kids started laughing because they thought I was joking. Finally one of them realized I was serious and ran across the hall to get help from a teacher. She responded by saying she couldn't help because her medical expertise only involved putting on Band-Aids.

Yes.... I finally hacked up the piece of granola bar and lived to tell this tale.

After Andy came in from recess one winter morning, he put his tongue on the hot radiator to demonstrate how steam is formed.

Carl (a 7th grader) was presenting his project to me and stopped and asked me, "Mrs. Fillip, is this topic over your head because I can slow down for you?"

Joey asked if there would be a grade on their report card for detention.

Laura did not do her grammar homework because she did not understand what an advective was. (Apparently that is new to me as well—maybe a cross between adjective and verb?)

CHAPTER FOUR

Say That Again?

"Kids say the darndest things."—Art Linkletter

Assigning projects can be a headache for students and parents. During my early years of teaching, I would assign a project and have the students do it at home. When I was teaching a life science course to seventh graders, their project assignment required them to work with plants or animals. One student in particular had a bit of trouble sticking to deadlines with assignments, homework and projects. On the due date, she came in with a box of mini rubber tree plants. When it was her turn to present, she told us she had grown some rubber tree plants from seeds in the past few weeks. In addition, she had watered them every day using a variety of liquids. Her critical thinking question was, "What would happen to the growth of rubber tree plants if they were hydrated with different liquids? It seemed like a reasonable experiment.

Listening to her presentation however, up popped the first red flag. She said she had grown these plants from seed. Indeed, they looked like they had grown from seed but they were about eight inches tall. It takes a long time to get rubber tree seedlings to sprout. After one week, rubber tree plants are only about 1-2 centimeters tall. She said they had been growing for a few weeks. They were much too tall and developed for that time period. Second red flag. All the plants looked the same. So rubber tree plants can grow in *any* liquid and survive with thick, green leaves? When I asked her what liquids she used, she paused and reeled off water, salt water, liquid fungicide, oil and few others. Amazing! All those plants survived from being hydrated with liquids other than water.

There was no data table to document her efforts. She concluded she was exempt from making a data table because all her plants looked the same, and did not respond differently to the liquids. Not to embarrass her on this feeble attempt of a project, I made a few comments such as, "Hmm, very interesting." (That's always a good one to use when you are sure this project grade is headed south.) I thanked her for the presentation and told her to put the plants on the window sill. When she went to lunch, I went over and picked up the plants to look at the bottom. Sure enough, there on the bottom was the name of the plant, the price tag and *yesterday's* date. Interesting. Did she honestly think I wouldn't notice? Today, ten years later, my rubber tree plant is about 18 inches tall, grown from one of her experimental plants.

* * *

During the years I taught U.S. history, my students embarked on a genealogy project. For many of the students, it was an enlightening experience. Many children have no clue where their ancestors come from. They think that generations back, their families *still* came from America. After the students had researched their heritage and put together a presentation, I invited parents and family members to our class to share in the presentations. I love it when kids do a presentation, make a faux pas and don't even realize it. Kelsey stood up to share her story and started off with, "I'm 50% Irish, 50% Italian, and 50% French." You could hear the chuckles throughout the room. At the conclusion of her talk, I told Kelsey I was thrilled with her efforts and so very glad to have 150% of her in my classroom this year.

* * *

Back in 1990, the Middle East was producing millions of barrels of oil a day. We began a discussion about this subject one day, and my students were suggesting the names of countries from the Middle East. Many countries such as Iraq and Iran came up. As the conversation ensued, we strayed off topic. I had someone ask me why the women in some of those countries had to wear a head and face covering. Being the teacher I am, I asked them why *they* thought the women did that. One student suggested it was to keep from smelling the oil. Another student said it was to keep them covered so other men could not see them and flirt with them. Then

I had a student who raised her hand to tell me she had been to Texas three times in her life and all she ever saw were men wearing cowboy hats. My immediate thought was this kid has had her head in a comic book for the last twenty minutes and has no clue what we are talking about. I paused for a minute and asked her, "What has Texas got to do with this conversation?" She looked at me like *I* was the dumb bunny and said, "Well, we are talking about the Middle East aren't we? Oil and stuff?" "Yes, we are," I said. "But I'm not seeing the connection between the Middle East, oil, and Texas. Can you help me out here?" The student looked at me with exasperation. "Mrs. Fillip, we live in the east right? So doesn't that make Texas the Middle East and like Hawaii or something the Far East?" It was all I could do to keep from bursting out laughing. She was dead serious. Talk about being geographically challenged.

* * *

I never cease to be amazed at how some students can be so bold without being pretentious. That's just the way they are: kids will say what's on their mind. I was idling in the hallway when I happened to overhear one of my students stop my principal to ask her a question. I loved this principal. She had a dry sense of humor and sometimes her stern look made you think she wasn't always happy with you. But if you looked closely, there was always a twinkle in her eye. I learned more from her than any other principal I ever had. Anyway, Elliot stopped her one day in the hallway and said, "Do you know why a lifesaver has a hole in the middle?" The principal paused for a minute and then said, "No Elliot, why is that?" Elliot continued explaining the hole was there in case you started choking. The hole would save you because you could breathe through the hole. The principal smiled and said, "Why thank you Elliot. I didn't know that." He looked at her for a minute and then said, "Well, it just goes to show you can teach old dog new tricks." After he walked away, the principal and I roared with laughter.

I REMEMBER WHEN...

A parent wrote me a note telling me that her son could not do the report on Stonewall Jackson because they could not find anything *anywhere* about stone walls during the Civil War.

Lilly got a piece of popcorn stuck in her nose and Freddy grabbed the tweezers we use for dissections to get it out.

Ali asked me if chocolate makes you horny.

I had to have a serious talk to the boys in my class about NOT farting.

Stephanie asked me in what country the Korean War was fought.

I told the kids the bonus question on the test was to answer who was buried in Grant's tomb. Amanda had a fit saying that was so unfair to ask that because we had only been learning about the explorers and had not yet gotten to the Revolutionary War.

CHAPTER FIVE

Other Points of View

"More important than the curriculum is the question of the methods of teaching and the spirit in which the teaching is given."—Bertrand Russell

When I moved to Massachusetts I switched gears from public high school to a private, Catholic school. The school was quite insular and its rules and regulations were counter to everything I experienced in a public school. The first day I sent them all off to lunch only to be reprimanded severely. Apparently I had forgotten the "lunch prayer" and they were to file out in a boys line and girls line *quietly* to the cafeteria. Oops! However, it was during this time I fell in love with middle school kids. I also realized kids are kids whether they are in public or Catholic schools. The students in the Catholic school were well behaved, disciplined in their studies, and overall very friendly. I really loved those kids. I was teaching math, science, history and literature. The curriculum was quite traditional but I was allowed to be creative and teach beyond the scope of required frameworks. I have fond memories of teaching there but the low salary drove me out and I had four kids of my own to put through college. During the time I was there, they were building a brand new charter school a few towns over. Branching out to a new and different professional experience sounded appealing. I relished the idea of being considered a founding faculty member. It would have been a first time opportunity. After nine years at the Catholic school I applied to the charter school and was accepted. Suddenly I had a summer job. Throughout July and August, the new faculty and staff spent time understanding how a charter school works. When I came on board, I was considered a veteran teacher. But I was greener than a stick when it came to my competency level in the design of an "essential" charter school. An essential school is a school where students are known personally, challenged intellectually, and expected to participate actively in their own learning. The school is guided by its commitment to diversity and inclusiveness. The school seeks to send graduates into the world who think for themselves, care about others, and act creatively and responsibly. They follow ten common essential principles such as, "student as worker, teacher as coach; demonstrate mastery through exhibition; and personalize teaching and learning. Never before I had been so integrated with the personal success of my students. Cross curriculums projects were mandated and that created such a cohesive team of teachers. My years teaching there were rewarding and enriching. Professionally, I grew tenfold.

Throughout all the schools I worked, there was a commonality among the students in regards to how they learn and how they behave which affected my philosophy as an educator. Kids needed me to be true to myself, be fair and be consistent. Being a teacher is a complex task but my own philosophy became such a strong model for the students. How I taught often became how they learned. Students study their teachers and we should make an effort as a teacher to study our students. Know your students! I can't remember what color pants I wore to work yesterday. But ask a student. They are incredibly observant. It's uncanny how they remember things I say that have nothing to do with positive learning. Students are impressionable and take your words to heart. I learned the hard way to be careful of sharing personal information with my students. I told a story in class of the time I cheated in class on a test when I was a student. The kids asked me why I did it. I told them I was irresponsible because I didn't study the night before and I was desperate. I made it a point to tell them this was *wrong* and I should have suffered the consequences of not studying. Kids hear want they want to hear! A few days later, I caught Tessa cheating on a test. When the principal spoke with her and asked her why she did it, Tessa responded, "Well, Mrs. Fillip said she cheated once." I wanted to disappear at that very moment.

In preparing this book, I found it interesting to talk to other people about education. Specifically, I interviewed teachers, students, and parents to learn their perspectives on teaching. The main thread that kept repeating itself was students and parents want to have competent teachers. While there is a general concern there is too much apathy among students today, kids who are well invested in their education want teachers who are intelligent. The importance of teachers getting to know their students was another reoccurring theme. Monica Bacon, who just graduated from North Middlesex Regional High School, in Townsend, Massachusetts, told me too many teachers talk "at" you and not "with" you. Personalizing the learning experience makes her more motivated. She liked having teachers tell the class something personal about themselves. She said it made them more human. Nicole Beauchesne, who will enter nursing school in the fall, said teachers who were excited about their teaching made her excited about her learning. And last, Nicole felt the notion of having to work hard to achieve something seems untouchable by too many kids. She said kids want things but don't want to work hard for them.

David is a junior at a high school in Massachusetts. He describes himself as an "Army brat." Because of the various places his father was stationed, David had the opportunity to go to school in Europe until 8th grade. He will attend school in Massachusetts until 12th grade. Compared to children who go to school in Europe, he observed students in the United States taking things for granted. He said many students don't want to work hard. They will just do the minimum. He suggested students think they are small and insignificant, and their contribution to the society doesn't matter. The country will go on. Another look at education comes from Noelle Nanto who is a junior at a public high school in Massachusetts. She feels people in this country are obsessed with making money. She knows in order to make money, you have to work hard. But that seems contrary to what kids want to do. They want to have tons of money but they don't want to work hard to get it. She feels that part of education is learning how to treat each other and how to get along. Life is all about relationships. She said people need to change their attitude toward one another. "Why can't we all get along?" said Noelle. The apathy about getting along with each other while maintaining a positive working environment leads her to believe too many people think individually they cannot make a difference. Noelle is trying to make that difference herself but thinks a group of people could be more effective. She quotes, "We all need to get educated about the problems and work together to solve them." Getting an education is important and we will benefit from that by having good teachers in the school who can help us about working together and how to be motivated."

What are some of the problems? What keeps kids from excelling? David believes children have too many outside activities. Cynthia, his mother, explained educational philosophy in Germany. Their philosophy is quite different from the U.S. When a German child is preparing to enter school, a school will ask the parents to name the single most important thing they can do to help the child get ready for school. A U.S. parent might respond and highlight the need to read out loud to a child. A German parent will say making sure children have ample time to play and have unstructured time. Germany starts school for youngsters in the first grade. They learn their numbers and letters but they do this in a four-hour school day. In fact, they go to school from 8 a.m. to noon every day for the first four years of their schooling. There is no kindergarten. When they arrive home for lunch, they have about one hour of homework. The rest of the time is for playing, being outside, and being a kid! When the students come back to school the next day, they are rested and stress-free.

I know with my own children, the idea of being in too many activities can become overwhelming. In the 2003 January issue of Psychology Today, the author says parents may feel remiss if their kids are not involved in a million activities. Perhaps they are compensating for all the things they couldn't do as a child. They want to give their children opportunities so they can grow up and look back with fond memories of everything they did. But there are more children who want to play outside, ride their bikes, and play in a tree fort. Loading them up with structured activities has stifled creativity and imagination. No question, as a child matures and ages, they should have the ability to handle a diversity of activities. Older children experience eustress which is the stress that makes people rise to the occasion and be successful. They enjoy the challenges that hard work can bring. It is the opposite of distress. But when they are young, they need time to be kids!

David had another thought on why kids today don't excel in their studies which results from students being unfocused. He said they don't show interest in what they are learning. He believes children don't see the big picture and don't realize what their school can give them. Nicole, a recent college graduate says she remembers too many students were satisfied with just a mediocre performance. There is a sense of pride when you do well and many kids believe they can't get there. While Nicole was self motivated, many students are not. Sara, a sophomore at a private school, says her school is constantly promoting school activities, but she said she thinks these programs are targeted for a specific group of kids. "Either you need to be a good athlete, a talented musician, have a passion for art, or be super smart," Sara explained. In a big high school there are many students who don't belong to any particular group. From my experience, practically every parent who was ever asked if they wanted their child to be in an after-school program said yes. Realistically, the school where I taught had about about 50% of the students doing an extra-curricular activity. David feels that students who don't get involved in *something* tend to lean toward unproductive behaviors such as engaging in drugs or drinking. Carla, a recent graduate, says teenage pregnancy is on the rise. Many of her friends have dropped out of school to have a baby then never go back. It's as though they don't believe in themselves any more.

Margaret Myers taught school in Washington D.C. for 25 years for grades one, two and three. Her school was bilingual. One teacher in the class taught in Spanish and the other teacher taught in English. Prior to teaching, Margaret was a Christian missionary. She said she became a teacher not only because she loves children, but because she thought she could be of service to inner city children. Margaret, now retired, enjoyed her teaching immensely and believed nothing else called her. When asked if she felt she made a difference, she offered this. "I like to think I helped some of my students become the successes they are in the world today." She went on to say knowing that information is hard to measure but hopefully she was an influence in one way or another.

Jeannie Erikson is a psychology teacher at a regional high school in Massachusetts. She also teaches career and life management, health, and transitions. She said she's been in the school system because she enjoys the relationships with the kids. I heard from Jeannie and other teachers that kids have tremendous potential but lack support at home. She said parents need to balance fostering independence while continuing to encourage their children to do their personal best. There is pressure for kids to succeed and the intensity to do well has increased. Getting into college is not a given like it was twenty years ago. Emily graduated from college five years ago. She agrees a lack of parental support is an issue, but on the flip side, felt an intense pressure from her parents to do well so she could achieve her career dreams. There needs to be a balance. Pressure or not, when I ask kids today where they want to be in ten years, more than half have no clue. Is there a solution?

In talking with students, I asked them what qualities make a good teacher. I found several threads of commonality among the answers. David said teachers need to be friendly and nice, but also commanding to motivate students. He also said they need to have a good sense of humor and have fun in the classroom. Nicole and Emily felt classroom control was a big factor. They felt it was unfair to punish an entire class for the behavior of a few. Teachers need to be creative, helpful, and patient. When I was working at the charter school, students told me it was very important to have teachers get to know them. This charter school had an advisory program where every teacher was assigned a group of students they met with every day. The idea was to create a relationship between those particular students and a teacher so that every student knew at least one adult well. If situations came up where a student needed to talk to an adult, they at least they knew their advisor. I thought the program was very effective.

Linda, another recent graduate was exasperated with MCAS exams (Standardized testing in Massachusetts). She thinks they are pointless. Her solution was to eliminate standardized tests and replace them with final exams. She doesn't believe MCAS tests have been successful in showing whether kids are learning more or doing better in school. Moreover, she remembers teachers being frantic about teaching the material for the MCAS. She noticed many of her teachers feeling tremendous pressure for their students to do well on their MCAS. This takes away from the true character of a teacher.

High school junior Kyle Sparkane wants teachers to spend more time preparing students for the world they'll face after they graduate. Many kids don't go to college and end up working after high school. But it's not because they aren't smart enough, it's because they can't afford it, Kyle says. "Who is teaching us how to get a job, or perform adequately at an interview?" he asked. It's not like we have this big resume we can hand the employer." He went on to say the most frustrating thing is not to be hired because we don't have experience. "How are we supposed to *get* the experience?"

Jeannie remarked that as a teacher she feels being creative is important. Teachers today need to know how to connect with kids. Being aware of individual learning styles compels her to use differentiated instruction techniques. Giving student's project options helps to motivate them. Lydia is a teacher at an elementary school. At times she becomes frustrated with the school system. While it is necessary to be creative, she feels hampered by a lack of materials. "The name of the game is budget, budget, budget." There is no magic formula to fix this problem. Ultimately, teachers spend hundreds of dollars of their own money to supplement their classes. The students are excited there might be cow eyeballs to dissect, but they are clueless as to who pays for them. "Students shouldn't have to worry where the money comes from to pay for supplies. However, the school barely can outfit the classroom anymore. In order to have effective and interesting science labs, I believe it was necessary to dip into my own wallet. Long gone are the days of reading the textbook and answering the questions at the end of the chapter," Linda said. To be an effective teacher, particularly a science teacher, you need to have supplies.

Carla is a student who easily becomes frustrated with teachers who don't know their subject well. She said that if they are getting paid to teach the material then there is no excuse for not knowing the subject. In addition, she dislikes teachers who try to impress the class with big vocabulary words or by talking over their heads. She says teachers need to keep it simple so students can understand the material. Furthermore, she has remarked that more often teachers seem to have trouble controlling the class. "How am I supposed to learn if students are misbehaving or distracting me?" she wondered. That theme kept popping up. Sara told me she felt it was important for teachers not to be so rigid with their curriculum. I can honestly say I was a teacher who took advantage of opportunities that went beyond the frameworks. I had read about Gene Simmons of the 70s rock group KISS. Gene used to be a high school teacher. He taught at a public school in Spanish Harlem while moonlighting for a career in music. His employment was somewhat tenuous. Apparently he went outside the box teaching English by using *Spiderman* comic books as teaching aids instead of using classic Western literature. Personally, the idea is not so radical. It all depends on how you use it. I worked in a school where the English teacher used comic strips and it was very effective.

The concept of going beyond the regular curricula occurred with a heartwarming incident that happened on an anniversary of 9/11. A student named Joanne said she was in homeroom when the principal came on the PA system and asked the school to stop for a minute to remember the events of that tragic day. When she came to my class later in the morning, I had a short presentation on my computer. It was a three-minute clip depicting several famous people like John Kennedy, Mother Theresa, and Albert Einstein. The image of each person was shown with one of their famous quotes. The clip was set to music and emotionally provocative. I told the kids to watch the presentation and pay close attention to the quotes. If possible, I wanted them to pick out a quote that seemed to have some meaning for them. At the conclusion of the presentation, there would be time to share their thoughts. The clip ended and I immediately had students who wanted to participate. Danny told the class he loved the quote from Walt Disney which said, "If you can dream it, do it." He remarked, too many people tell other people what or what not to do in life. He remembered his parents talking about 9/11 at the time and said that

President Bush told the nation we wouldn't give in to terrorism. He made an analogy between the attack on the twin towers and Walt Disney's quote. Danny was distraught the people who worked in the Twin Towers woke up in their homes, went to work, and never knew it was going to be their last day. He wondered how many of them might have wished they had done other things in their lives if they had known it was going to be their last day here on Earth. Danny told the class we need to live each day to the fullest because you never know when it might be your last day. If you have a desire or dream to do something, then you shouldn't wait. More children joined in the discussion and contributed significant thoughts and ideas. There was a strong and powerful spirit in the classroom. The class never did their regularly scheduled class work. Nobody cared either. The emotional feeling of what had happened on 9/11 stayed with those students. But more importantly, they were inspired by this one quote to become whatever they wanted to be in life. It was one of the most enriching class discussions I have ever had as a teacher. And it all happened because I took a chance and went "outside the box."

* * *

Being a teacher gives me the prerogative to provide learning opportunities outside the classroom. When my own children were very young, my husband and I would rent a house or condo during the summer by the ocean or up at Lake Winnipesaukee in New Hampshire. We realized during these trips there might be a time that just my husband and I wanted to do something *alone*, without the kids. Our son was not old enough to babysit his younger siblings. The remedy was to bring along a high school teenager to watch our kids when my husband and I wanted some break time.

One summer we rented a house in Mattapoisett, which is on the southern shore of Massachusetts. Mattapoisett is a small ocean-side community of about 7000 people. Boaters flock to a body of water near there known as Buzzards Bay. The bay is great for sailing as one can always count on an 11:00 southwest breeze just about every summer day. The ocean is great for swimming due to a wonderful sandy bottom and mostly rock-free beaches. The Gulf Stream works its way up into the bay, making the temperature of the ocean in the 70s and even low 80s.

We chose Jamie to accompany us one summer as we headed down to Mattapoisett. Jamie was born and raised in Vermont. At the tender age of 15, she had never traveled outside of Vermont in her entire life. When I asked her if she wanted to come with us, she was ecstatic. My brief description of Mattapoisett let Jaime know the town was west of Cape Cod. She nodded as though she completely understood. She told me she couldn't wait to get home and check it out on the map. Apparently, over the next few weeks, Jaime told several people she was traveling with Mrs. Fillip and her family to another country over the summer. I was unaware she had been telling people this story. Bess, a history teacher, stopped me one afternoon and asked me what country I was traveling to that summer. At first, I was confused and then laughed, thinking she thought Mattapoisett was another country. Not understanding my humor, Bess told me Jamie had told her she was going to a foreign country with Mrs. Fillip over the summer. "Really!" I said. I was perplexed why Jaime was telling everyone that. I found Jamie at the end of the day and casually asked if she knew where Cape Cod was? "Oh yes," she said, "I looked on the map and I see it is down there at the bottom of Africa." Wow! I'm not sure what map she was looking at, but she was confusing Cape Cod with the Cape of Good Hope. Another geographically challenged student!

We took Jamie to Mattapoisett, not Africa, and her small world opened up despite the geographical difference. She had never been swimming in the ocean and she informed us she wouldn't be swimming for fear of sharks. The last time a shark had ever ventured into Buzzards Bay and bitten someone was in 1936. By the last day of our vacation, we couldn't get her out. Even so, she still wouldn't partake of our clambake. My husband and I were "monsters" for putting those poor lobsters into a steaming pot of water. I'm not sure what category the "butcher" fell under as she chowed down her hamburger while we were eating our succulent lobsters. Every summer thereafter we took a different girl with us on our trips. It gave me tremendous satisfaction to give these kids an opportunity to get out of Vermont. Maybe we didn't travel the world, but going two states south of Vermont seemed like the other side of the world to them. I appreciated their help and they appreciated the adventure.

I REMEMBER WHEN . . .

Joanna asked me if my mother had children.

I was reprimanding Harold and using his name a few times during my reprimand. When I finished I asked him if he had anything to say. "Yes, Mrs. Fillip. My name is William."

Becky got a 100% on her test and Jim insisted she tell him how she did that. Becky got so mad she yelled, "I ate a bag of Smarties before the test."

Jim actually tried that before the next test.

Megan thought the word MAFIA stood for "Mothers and Fathers Italian Association." She then went on to tell me that I could not be a member because I had blonde hair and blue eyes.

Jason and Phil filled my wastebasket with water and then piled a bunch of papers on the top. Later in the day, I noticed the basket was filled to the brim, so I put my foot in the waste basket to push down the papers.

You know what happened next!!!!!!!!!!!!!!

Travis put gorilla glue on one of my lab stools and Tyler sat on it. The only way Tyler could get off the stool was to step out of his pants. (I had some serious explaining to do to Tyler's mom)

CHAPTER SIX

How Long is Your Fuse?

"Experience is a hard teacher because she gives the test first, the lesson afterward."—Vernon Law

One afternoon while teaching math, a huge thunderstorm rolled through our area. It was a torrential downpour. Huge claps of thunder and lightning bolts were everywhere and zapped the school on the far side of the building from where I was teaching. I was unaware this had happened but the wire going from the outside of the school into a storage room started to smolder. Right on cue, the fire alarm went off. At first, we all sat, and were shocked (So much for the fire drill practices we had). The first reaction to the fire alarm is to get out of the building. But we just sat there hearing the rain and thunder. We couldn't imagine the firemen would actually have us *exit* the building. I poked my head out of the classroom and saw my principal walking across the lunch area. I inquired as to whether we had to get out. As soon as I saw the reaction on her face, I knew we were going. "Move," she said. "If the alarm goes off you must get out." Incredulous, I turned to the class and told them to get up and file out quietly and orderly. As we moved toward the doors, I could hear students exclaiming in disbelief that we actually had to go outside. I was thinking the same thing. My brain was calculating what kind of punishment would be suitable for the jerk that pulled the alarm during a thunderstorm.

This was no ordinary rain storm. The street had become so flooded, water was gushing over the top of the front steps and into the building. As we approached the door, and saw torrents of water gushing into the building, I had several students who were visibly frightened. They didn't want to go out. I must admit, I wasn't real thrilled myself. It was a toss-up. Get burned up in the building or burned up by a lightning bolt. Tough choice. As we approached the threshold of the door a seventh grader suddenly balked. She wouldn't step outside with me. She clung to me and started crying, telling me she was scared to death. I looked at her and saw the terror in her eyes. Calmly I told her we *had* to go and she would be safe. I mean, how did I know that? All I knew was I had to get those kids out of the building. She was solid as a plow horse standing in the doorway. Kids started to pile up behind us. "Come on," they yelled. "Keep the lines moving." I couldn't get her to move. Gently I tried to convince her that I would protect her from the lightning as if I was going to carry a steel rod and have the lightning deflect from her onto me. I could feel my own panic as the kids behind me started to push and shove. I could not get her to move her feet. Talk about a lesson in patience! I didn't want to get mad but I didn't know how to get her out the door short of picking her up and carrying her. Finally, I took her arm and gently but robotically guided her one step at a time until we were outside. Immediately we were pelted by slanting rain. I could hear the thunder crashing and see the lightning flashes as we waddled our way through puddles. After we exited the building, we turned right and crossed over the bridge to the designated spot where we go for fire drills. The bridge has steel handrails and kids were holding onto them as they crossed over. Any minute I expected to see one of them burst into flames. Above the roar of the rain and thunder, I yelled to them to let go of the handrails. I doubt anyone heard me. We made it to our safety zone, which was a parking lot with plenty of metallic cars sitting around. We waited for the fire department as many terrorized seventh graders huddled around me. I tried to protect them. Many were crying and, in my need to make them feel safe, I forgot about my own fear. The process of checking the school for safety took 15-20 minutes. I watched other students trying to comfort their frightened friends. We learned a lesson in patience as we endured the horrific storm. Kids and teachers were whining about wanting to go back inside. When the coast was clear, we paraded back into the building, soaked to the skin. Everyone was sent home except the staff. Apparently, there had been a guest speaker from another state who arrived earlier waiting to present a program for the staff. He was in his car when the fire alarm went off. The staff was required to stay—in our soaking wet clothes and dripping hair. What a sight we must have been!

Experience has taught me that teaching can be a constant struggle to maintain patience. My goal as a teacher is to inspire and encourage kids to think. I'm supposed to do this and maintain a high level of patience throughout the *entire* day. Of course I don't have the extreme situation of worrying about being fried in a cloudburst every single day. But each day I must engage in the art of patience. It's not something taught in a textbook. Patience evolves over time. I believe teachers come on board somewhere in the middle of the patience scale. As I reflect back on my own experience, years and years of sitting in the room with teachers, I am aware every teacher has a finish line for patience. One morning I might wake up feeling exhausted or not feeling well. The thought of climbing back under the covers is so tempting. But I manage to pull myself together and make it to school on time. Despite how lousy I feel, when the students arrive, I paste that smile on my face and begin my day. This is one of the reasons I love the weekends. I don't have to pretend for anyone. If I want to be grumpy, I can! On those tough days, I'm always tempted to alert my students that I'm not in a great mood—so don't try my patience. But it didn't seem fair. I know many kids come to school with issues from home that keeps them from having any patience with me. I wouldn't allow them to use that as an excuse for being rude or disrespectful. So why should I be any different. The question you might ask yourself is, how long is your fuse?

Kids today want everything, all the time, and they want it *now*. The idea of instant gratification is prevalent and patience is something students need to be taught. All day I have students clamoring for my help. How many times a day do I tell a student they have to wait? One of me, so many of them. Sometimes I think my students feel like they are patients in the emergency room and their issue is so acute they need me now! In the course of one class, I may have to individually help several students. It seems, at times, necessary to have forty eyes in my head so I can see what everyone is up to. If this is an unstructured class such as a science lab, I need radar and echolocation. Organization was the key to my success for keeping my patience level at a minimum. When doing a class that involved several pieces of equipment and safety was a factor, keeping kids on task and knowing where everything and everyone was became imperative. If I was organized, I could place my attention on the needy students and not worry so much about the others.

It always amazes me that I can be talking with someone and kids will just come up and start talking to me like there was nobody there. Don't they see I am yakking away with someone else? Finally, not being able to avoid the persistent student, I tell them I will be with them shortly. "But my question is important," they say. Using my discretion to put the other person on hold for this dire emergency is mostly done to prevent a lawsuit. I mean, maybe the kid just swallowed some calcium chloride and is wondering why his lip is swelling up like a balloon. *Usually* it's something another student could answer such as, "Do we hold the paper vertical or horizontal?" Making my students aware of the customary phrase "excuse me" can only be modeled for students if I demonstrate patience and courtesy myself. Otherwise, I become a hypocrite. How do I expect kids to learn the skill of patience if I lose mine just because they interrupted me? I am fully aware it is impossible for me to reach into myself and create a Zen moment every time I get irritated with a student. As Kathy Christie said, "Teachers are people too. They can lose patience just as well as anyone else. Everyone's got their level of tolerance. Even the best of folks can lose it now and then."

There is one infamous question students ask that makes me go crazy. When kids are doing an assignment or taking a test, they ask me if spelling counts. I mean, *what kind of question is that?* "Oh sure, spell however you want today because it doesn't matter if metamorphic is spelled R-E-T-I-R-E-M-E-N-T because I will know *exactly* what you are talking about." Come on. How do they expect me to answer? I mean, wouldn't you *want* to spell the words as correctly as possible *all* the time? If I said it doesn't count today, will they purposely try to spell the words wrong? So if spelling *does* count, in theory kids will actually access their brain cells a little harder to try and spell the words correctly. What a concept! Spelling today is atrocious. I attribute this to kids using spell check on computers. They don't have to know how to spell anymore because the computer points out their mistakes and fixes them. But when they are handwriting something, they are the computer! They have to come up with the proper spelling and sometimes that is just *too much effort*. So the question, "does spelling count?" really tries my patience. The side effects of losing one's patience can often be sarcasm. I confess this is my one defining weaknesses. "Sure," I tell the kids. "Spell however you want today. Take a vacation from using your brain cells."

Ultimately, school should be a safe haven for learning and allowing students to make mistakes without reproach. That can make for a long day. If my first period class made me feel like I just went through a wind tunnel, the degree of patience begins to drop early in the day. I look at my teaching schedule for the rest of the day and realize my most difficult group of kids comes last period. Groan! On a Friday! Double groan! I know this will be a very long day. Maybe somebody made extra, extra, chocolate chip cookies for lunch. I will need them! Sometimes I think about my level of patience and how this plays a part in a student's life down the road. When you get to be my age, the first set of kids I taught are now well immersed in the working world. Someday I might run into one of those students where I need their help. Or worse, I might be their patient. Suppose I had an accident that required me to get stitches. I see the doctor and then he announces his assistant will stitch me up. In walks Gloria. "Oh my goodness. Gloria? You're a physician's assistant now? That's wonderful. I am so proud of you." Gloria looks at me with that plastic, professional smile but deep down inside she remembers those days in my classroom where every other word coming out my mouth was, "*Gloria, stop talking. Gloria, if I have to speak to you one more time, I am going to have to move your seat. Gloria, I have given you several opportunities to be in the classroom without disrupting the other students. Obviously you cannot seem to do that today. Gloria, I need you to leave the room and see the principal.*" By the time I utter that last statement, I hardly notice my voice has risen, my fists are slightly clenched, and deep down inside I am happy to have Gloria take a little break from my classroom. Okay. I admit it. There are times I have been relieved that a student trying my patience has been removed from the room. How many of us have started a sentence in our head with, "If that kid does that one more time . . . ?" We all know what we would *like* to do, but we never do it. Meanwhile, Gloria picks up the needle and thread and the sun picks up the glint of revenge in her eyes. I hold my breath and wait.

I REMEMBER WHEN . . .

Sarah served animal crackers to the class. She told us they were chocolate. Lots of comments were made how delicious they were and how "chocolately" they tasted. Later we found out she had colored them all with a brown magic marker. Ahhh . . . . the power of suggestion.

Emily asked if "quizzical" is a fancy word for quiz like test is short for "testicle."

I was demonstrating the eye wash in the science lab and then asked for a volunteer to be a "victim." Ryan jumped up and stuck his face right into the eye wash. Not wanting to get water everywhere, I told him that was enough. Before he got his head completely out of the eyewash, I started to close it up and whacked the metal door right up his nose. Poor bloke. He had to go to the nurse with a bad, bloody nose.

Yes . . . I still was able to keep my job.

Before we took our trip to the Court House, I was trying to demonstrate how a courtroom was set up. Looking for good props to show the arrangement of a courtroom, I grabbed the nativity set (Baby Jesus, Mary, Joseph, angels, shepard's, etc) that had been set up for Christmas. Drawing his own analogy between Jesus being born in a manger because there was no room at the inn, Lyle asked me if babies were born in the court room because there was no room at the hospital. (I'm not kidding. He was dead serious)

CHAPTER SEVEN

You *Have* to Laugh

"There will rarely be genuine and healthy laughter in the classroom unless the teacher can laugh at a number of things in general, and at himself in particular." Anonymous

On my teaching evaluations, principals always wrote I was an enthusiastic teacher. And I was because I had a passion for teaching, but I also had a good sense of humor. Holding true to the belief you can be educated while having fun, I laugh at situations that would have given teachers a convulsion 25 years ago. A sense of humor is absolutely necessary when teaching. At times class can be very intense. Serious learning is going on! I feel like I'm connecting with my students and some wonderful things are happening. Frequently I will bring up some concept or topic I taught the previous day. Let me ask you. What happens from the time kids go home at the end of the day to when they come back the next? Is there a magic wand the size of the universe that magically erases all the knowledge you taught them on Monday, so by Tuesday it's gone? One day I was talking about the previous day's lesson on nutrition when I asked *anyone* in the room if they can remember a particular vocabulary term I taught them. Dead silence. No response. First I wonder if anyone has plugged in their memory cells. No takers. Maybe I should be doing a pulse check to see if they are actually breathing. Finally I give a hint. "It begins with the letter F." Again, I get no response. Even the brainier kids are staring back at me with glazed eyes. I try another hint, "It has something to do with me." Finally, a voice from the back of the room yells out, "fat." Time stands still for one moment. "You could have heard a pin drop" was never truer at this moment. Now remember, I had been doing a unit on nutrition. The consequences of eating too many simple carbohydrates could lead a person to become overweight. It was not a mystery I love my sweets which helped to add a few extra pounds to my body. The kids in the room felt comfortable enough with me and knew I was "always trying to lose weight." So the comment about me being fat couldn't be taken as malicious. Twenty-five faces looked at me to see how I would respond. I'm sure half the kids thought the brave student was done for. It was a defining moment for me. I could have easily been insulted and lost my cool. Instead, I burst out laughing and said at least he was honest. The class bursts out laughing as well. We all got a good chuckle and as I tell that story to other teachers they are amazed I could laugh. Why not? Learning in the classroom goes far beyond textbooks and worksheets. Teaching kids to laugh at themselves in certain situations is a survival tool for life. There was nothing to do but laugh. When I see these kids years later, they still bring up that story.

* * *

During my eighth grade unit on weather catastrophes, Ryan and Matt were doing a project on tsunamis. Their plan was to bring a rain gutter into class to demonstrate the rise and fall of a tsunami wave. When it was their time to present, they left the classroom and told me they were fetching their supplies. After what seemed like an extraordinarily long time, I heard a raucous going on down at the bottom of the stairwell. I scooted outside the room and looked over the railing to the stairs below. To my amazement, I saw Ryan and Matt trying to carry a rain gutter up three flights of stairs, full of water! As they rounded the corner and started to walk up the third flight, Matt lost his grip. The gutter began to tilt wildly and all the water gushed out right into the front office. It was just my luck the principal happened to be in the office at the time. What a mess! Just as I expected, I heard my name carry up the stairs as the principal blasted through her megaphone, "Mrs. Fillip, we have a problem down here." Racing down the stairs, I saw water everywhere. Trying to sound authoritative in front of the principal, I sternly told the boys to get paper towels immediately and start cleaning up the mess. The principal looked at me incredulously. "Mrs. Fillip, I think we need a wet vac!" The boys and I went off in search of the custodian. As I explained to the boys that bringing the gutter up *empty* and getting water from the third floor bathroom would have made more sense, I couldn't help but chuckle.

* * *

I was teaching in Vermont and had an incredible team of science teachers. We all helped each other out with ideas. After talking with another physics teacher, I asked him if he had any ideas for projectile motion I could use for a demonstration in class as we were going to be building catapults and trebuchets. He was more than enthusiastic in helping me. In fact, he told me to bring in my class last period to watch a ten minute demo as he was doing projectile motion as well. Last period I brought my group in and we all lined up against the back wall. This particular physics teacher was well known for some theatrical demonstrations but nothing prepared me for what I was about to see. After a brief presentation on projectile motion, he showed us the plate of succotash he had eaten earlier. Succotash is a combination of corn and lima beans. Apparently when he was finished eating, he had swallowed the contents of a small bottle of Ipecac syrup. Ipecac syrup is a medicine that causes vomiting. In the past it was used to partially empty a person's stomach after a poison had been ingested. It is rarely used today. At this point, it had been about fifteen minutes since he swallowed the syrup. It takes about twenty to thirty minutes for Ipecac to take full effect. All the class knew (including me) is that he had eaten a plate of succotash.

We were ready to begin. "Ladies and gentlemen," the teacher said. "I am about to demonstrate for you a very unique performance of projectile motion. One you most likely will never forget." With that being said, he placed a large trash barrel about five feet away from himself. Hanging from the lab table were two large strips of duct tape. Grabbing them with gusto, he placed them across his lips so they were sealed tightly. Then he faced the barrel and waited. We waited. You could hear sighs and giggles in the room. One student cynically said, "Oh yea, this is fun." Suddenly the teacher pitched forward slightly. You could the room respond with nervous anticipation. Then he pitched forward again but his face became very red. He reached out with his arm to steady himself against the lab table. Immediately his body convulsed again, his head jerked forward, and both arms grabbed the lab table. His body now heaved in a huge convulsion. Simultaneously, substances began to fly out of his nose in a projectile fashion. It was so grotesque it was mesmerizing. Corn, lima beans, snot, and liquid were shooting across the room into the barrel for the most part. Some of it was hitting the floor. The students sitting in the front row were leaping like gazelles to get out of the way. The teacher looked as though he was being strangled with a nylon cord. It is a visual I don't want to remember and I can imagine many students have trouble with it as well. The kids were screaming, laughing, gasping, gagging, and a few were throwing up themselves. It was pandemonium. It was so chaotic I could have cared less for a minute how the teacher was faring. I was too worried about the students. When the dust started to settle, I glanced over to the front of the room. The teacher was washing his face in the sink. A few kids had gone off to the nurse and others to get drinks. I think I was shell-shocked. Never in my entire career have I ever seen anything so bizarre. I took the class back to my room and we all sat down. The kids just looked at me. It was very quiet. I announced, "I won't be doing that as a demo any time soon." Nobody said anything for a minute. Then a student said, "He was right. We won't ever forget that performance." Slowly a few smiles started to creep up the sides of their mouths. I knew they would be okay.

* * *

During my career, I was fortunate to have the opportunity of being a mentor. In my first year at the charter school, my principal told me she knew this guy who was looking to become a teacher. He was part of the New Teacher's Collaborative, a yearlong program for aspiring teachers. But at the time she provided me few details. Because we were a new school, I walked into the room on the first day looking around since no one really knew anyone else. I was looking around for a young, spunky, college graduate. After a few minutes, a tall, lanky man with salt and pepper hair came over to me. "Hi," he said. "I'm Jack and I guess you are going to be my student teacher." I was shocked. Never did I expect to mentor a 43-year-old man. He had been an engineer for years and decided to change careers. We hit it off instantly. Jack and I worked together as a team and his expertise as an engineer added so much to my curriculum. I was able to offer my expertise on being a teacher. For the first three months, our students thought we were married, even though we had different names. The first day he was absent from school, the kids in my class asked me where my husband was. I never assumed the kids thought we were hubby and wife. When Jack came to school the next day, and told him the kids were concerned about where my "husband" was yesterday. We both cracked up laughing.

* * *

The tops of the cabinets in my science lab were stuffed full of boxes and other science equipment. I was tall enough to reach them if I stood on the lab table but it involved a two-step process. And I needed to be wearing pants, not a skirt. I was doing a physics lab that required us to use spring scales. A spring scale is simply a spring that's fixed at one end with a hook to attach an object to at the other. The force needed to extend a spring is proportional to the distance that spring is extended from its rest position. The scale markings on the spring scale are equally spaced. Seeing how the scales were in a box perched on the shelf above the cabinets, I asked for a volunteer to climb up and retrieve the box for me. *Normally*, a person would get a chair, drag it over to the lab table, step on the chair and then step onto the lab table. The tallest boy in the room could easily reach the box. But no! As I said before, always expect the unexpected. Danny quickly volunteered to climb up there to get the box. Out of my peripheral vision, I saw him take a running start from across the room and hurdle right up onto the four foot tall lab table from the floor. I gasped. There wasn't even time to stop him. After landing on the table, he proceeded to squat down in a style similar to how chimpanzees sit. He was laughing. Without hesitating, I grabbed the banana sitting on my desk and threw it to him. Everyone cracked up laughing. Especially Danny.

* * *

The decision to hatch chickens in the room came easy for me when I had several students in the room offering to take them home. The first time I had chickens, I made it clear to the kids it was essential I had a note from their parent approving the transport of a chicken to their home. Weeks went by and finally, with huge excitement, we watched all the chickens come out of their shells. Chick eggs need to be in a ninety-nine degree incubator for about twenty-one days. A week after they hatched, each student who had permission took their tiny, fuzzy, creature home. John had a note from a parent that said it was fine for him to take home six chickens. I loaded him up with six chickens and sent him home. The next morning I got to school and the principal was waiting to greet me. "Oh no," I thought. "What have I done this time?" She took me into her office and there was John, his father, and six chickens. John's father was livid. "What's the idea of sending my son home with live chickens?" he spits out. My immediate response was going to be, "Did you want them all cooked instead of alive?" But he was too angry to be funny. I took a deep breath and explained that I received a note from John's mother approving the transport of six chickens to their home. "Let me see the note," John's father demanded. As I walked back to my classroom to get the note (I always keep notes written from home in a folder in the event of a catastrophe such as this) it suddenly dawned on me that maybe John had *someone else* write this note. Upon returning to the office with the note, my amazing detective skills proved to be correct. John's fathered looked at the note and said, "That's not my wife's handwriting." Sure enough, clever John had his sister write the note. Poor John. He begged his dad to let him keep the chickens. Nope! John's father said there is no room at their house for chickens even though John insisted he could keep them in his bedroom. Six chickens, a disheartened John, and I shuffled back to my classroom. As for me, when I was brave enough to do chickens again, every hand written note was followed up with a phone call to the parent. "Did you order some chickens?"

* * *

In the middle of a class discussion, I noticed Terry kept turning her back to me. Without disrupting the flow of my class, I tried to figure out exactly what Terry was doing. After four times of deliberately putting her back to me, I said, "Terry, do you think you could please sit facing the front so I know you are on board with me? She never turned around and said with a hint of irritation in her voice, "Can you give me one more minute Mrs. Fillip? I'm trying to put on some mascara." I was taken aback. That had to be a first! "Well, by all means. Don't let me interrupt your beauty regimen."

* * *

One of the schools where I taught had a wonderful playground for the students. Someone decided it would be really neat to paint a huge map of the United States right on the black top. They did a superb job with a variety of colors and every state was labeled. Every morning, before school, the teachers rotated for morning duty on the playground. One gorgeous, fall morning I was standing out there doing my morning duty when a second grader came running over to me and said, "Mrs. Fillip, Mrs. Fillip, Ryan is throwing up on Texas." For a minute, it did not register. "Was there a student here named Texas?" Then I realized what she meant. As luck would have it, I turned around just in time to see Ryan heave again right onto the map. Oh yuck. Reluctantly, I walked over to the map, and Ryan was done vomiting. He looked up at me and said, "Hey Mrs. Fillip, good thing I didn't throw up on Delaware because I would have covered it all, right?" Hmm, yes, that's exactly what was going through my mind also.

* * *

All women fear this might happen to them some day. After doing my business in the ladies room, I wrestled with my pantyhose, put myself back together and walked down the hallway to my classroom. Suddenly from behind, I heard this strange sound. I turned and saw a young boy student staring at me with eyes as big as saucers. He immediately turned and bolted right into the principal's office. Curious that something terrible had just happened to this little boy, I went back down the hallway to the principal's office. As I walked in, I could see the doe-eyed boy looking at me again, very strangely. He spoke not a word. The principal and I looked at each other with, "What's going on?" I turned my back to the principal, bent over and asked the boy if he was okay. Then I heard a gasp from the principal. I looked up as she approached me. Quickly and almost violently she spun me around. I was escorted out of the office. The principal looked uncomfortable. "Ahem," she started. "The back of your skirt is completely tucked into your pantyhose. Your undies are there for the world to see." I was mortified. I quickly reached around to rectify the situation. My face was burning. And what about that little boy? I bet that poor little guy is still having nightmares.

* * *

At some point in my teaching career, I had to teach health. We had been talking about dental hygiene and eventually the conversation got around to wisdom teeth. Everyone was saying how uncomfortable it was to have your teeth extracted. I told the students that usually an oral surgeon takes care of such things. I just assumed everyone knew what an oral surgeon was. Rule number one: never assume! I saw a hand go up for a question and this young girl asked, "Where does the dentist stand when the operation is going on?" I said, "What do you mean?" She asked again, "Where does the dentist stand when he is giving directions to the surgeon?" I paused and tried to understand her question. Then I realized what she was thinking. She actually thought an oral surgeon literally meant someone was calling out directions while someone else operated. Wouldn't that be an interesting concept?

I REMEMBER WHEN...

Jake asked me if priests were allowed to pray or were just suppose to tell people to pray.

The students were assigned a project in religion class that required them to carry around a bag of flour that simulated a real baby. Never once were they allowed to leave their "baby" unattended. One morning when I came to class I saw that Ginny was missing her "flour baby." She handed me a note from her mom.

"Dear Mrs. Fillip. Ginny does not have her flour baby today because I accidentally turned her baby into bread. Sorry."

Jenna told me she had the hiccups and she needed to go to the nurse to get a Band-aid.

Brandon thought "Butox" (really Botox) was to make your butt less smelly.

I caught Ariana, Crystal, and Kaylynn playing poker and they were using real money. Their defense was they were practicing their math skills I had taught them.

Zoe asked me what kind of punishment the people got back in Isaac Newton's time if they did not follow his "Laws of Gravity."

CHAPTER EIGHT

Taking Risks but Never Cheat

I always try my best to make sure I'm putting across the curriculum in a way so every child can be inspired. Anatole France once said, "nine-tenths of education is encouragement."

When my own daughter was in high school, I had the opportunity to take over her math class. The class's track record of doing well academically and behaving was low on the spectrum. On my first day I asked the class why they felt they were doing so poorly. I was shocked at their response. "Well, we're the dumb class." "We hate math and every teacher who comes in here knows it." "We're never gonna use this stuff so why bother trying." "I don't get math and I feel stupid." Too bad they didn't have Socrates as a teacher. He believed that everybody already has true knowledge within their brain somewhere. The kids in this math class were *not* stupid. Math may have been a struggle for them, but I was convinced they had talked themselves out of believing they had any ability. My job the first few weeks was to build up their self-esteem in class. As time went by, I could hear the students saying things like, "That's not so hard. I can do this." Knowledge is power. These kids needed a nudge and encouragement from me. When I started the class, more than half the class was failing. When we finished the school year, only two students failed and that was because they *chose* to fail.

I want my students to try, to ask questions, and to take risks—even when I see answers on a test telling me that Leif Erikson landed on the coast of Colorado. It bothers me when students just give up and don't even try. In my advanced placement biology class, there was a student named

Kirk who was forced to take my class by his parents. In an act of retaliation, he drew cartoons in his notebook during my lectures, never handed in one homework assignment, and wrote the word "grapefruit" for every single answer on his test. Obviously he was trying to fail to send his parents a message. He sat in the back row and never bothered me or anyone else. Incidents like that were exceptions to the rule. Creating a classroom where it is safe to ask and answer questions is crucial. I know what happens when the teacher asks if anyone in the room doesn't understand something. The whole class holds its breath. So again, I ask if there is anyone who doesn't understand the material? Usually a hand timidly goes up. I don't hear the groan from the class but I can feel it. My students know better because I have repeated several times we *all* need to be respectful of those students who need extra help. There are probably five others who need to ask the same question. The smart teacher will re-teach the material for those who need it and let the others go on. My ultimate goal is this; "A teacher is one who makes himself progressively unnecessary." ~Thomas Carruthersching

* * *

When I was a little girl, I was standing next to my father at the local phone booth while he was making a call. After he was done, he hung up and the dime he had deposited came back. He picked up the dime and put it back into the phone. "What did you do that for?" I exclaimed. "We just got our dime back." My father turned to me and told me the dime belonged to the phone company because we had used their services. His lesson that day has remained with me for a long time. Whenever I think about being less than honest, I am reminded of my father's integrity. He was a role model for me. The same way I need to be a role model for my students. Unfortunately, when students are not motivated and are desperate to get good grades, they turn to less-than-honest behaviors such as cheating.

During the time I taught at a Catholic school, the opening part of homeroom was used to recite some prayers. From time to time, I would give the students a prayer they could tape to their desks so in the morning they would have it in front of them. The ultimate goal was to have them memorize the prayer. After a few weeks I told them part of their religion grade would be to write this prayer on a test. The day of the test came. I asked them all to remove their prayers from the tops of their desks. The test was distributed and I told them to write the prayer from memory on the back side of the test. I have to admit, I was somewhat naïve about cheating.

After teaching high school and dealing with cheating problems there, I thought middle school kids probably wouldn't dare cheat.

Everyone finished the test and handed them in. A bit later, a student came to me and told me she noticed Thomas didn't take the prayer off his desk. I thanked her and said I would deal with it later. Frankly, I was shocked. Kids cheat in my room? When the kids came back to my classroom after lunch, I announced that I had observed a student cheating on the prayer part of the test. I never told them *how* I saw them cheating. The old reverse psychology. It does work sometimes! I offered a chance for that student to come to me by the end of the day to confess they had been cheating. As the afternoon wore on, one by one, students came to my desk to tell me they cheated and how they did it!! I was amazed at how clever these kids were. I was so naïve. Thanks to all these dishonest (or desperate) kids, I learned several new ways to cheat. In the end, seven students came to me who admitted they had cheated. Thomas was not one of them!

In school, cheating is rampant. Half of this book could be devoted to cheating. According to The Mark Kula Center for Applied Ethics, over 70% of students today admit to cheating. But what constitutes cheating and what doesn't have become fuzzy for many students. There are many variables that incite students to cheat. Students will put pressure on themselves to excel and will resort to cheating. They want to maintain the highest grade point average in the class. Parents put pressure on their children to do well. Top grades equal better schools for college which equal better jobs or careers. Many students don't want to put in the time and effort to do quality work. Why do all the research when you can download a paper off the Internet? One of the buzz words I use in my classroom is integrity. It seems to me that if I concentrate my efforts on students being more honest rather than disciplining students for cheating, I get better results.

Lessons in integrity don't have to be huge. They start with small things. On the first day of class we talk about honesty. Honesty is a reflection of their character. For example, I tell my students I will assign homework four nights a week. The amount of time needed to do this work should take about 30 minutes. If the students need to spend more than thirty minutes on the assignment, they may stop working and get additional time the next night. We talk about the 30 minutes of *uninterrupted* time. No stopping for snacks, feeding the dog, talking on the phone, watching a bit of TV and so forth. This is where integrity plays a big part. It's a chance to use the honor system. In all my years of teaching I have never had a student take advantage of this. Just as I have to trust my students, it takes them time to trust I'll be consistent on this. Experience has taught me the older the student, the more cheating is prevalent. That's not to say cheating doesn't happen in first grade. But cheating is more than just copying answers off someone else's test. It carries over into other arenas like sports, relationships, and with parents.

Many of you probably remember the game, **Chutes and Ladders?** When one of my children would drag that out from the cabinet, I usually tried to pawn the game off on my husband. I had to practice *too much* patience when playing. If you have played this game, you might remember what happens. You and your child are moving along and you almost get to "The End." Inevitably you or your child hit one of the "chutes" and have to slide way back to the beginning. Groan! As the game progresses, I desperately try to get my child to the end. When they are near the finish they always seem to hit the chute again. Before they zoom back to the beginning and delay this game 15 more innings, I say, "I think you miscounted, honey. You should be on the *next* square because you had to move five squares." Of course the next square allows them to advance three more squares which bring this game to a finish. I rationalize this type of cheating as a necessity to preserve my sanity. But it isn't honest. Then one day I get caught because my kids got smarter. "No mom. I was on *this* square when I started and seven squares from that put me on the chute." Whoosh. We start all over again. Oh well, that game was better than Monopoly.

Teaching integrity begins at home. Unfortunately, these lessons don't happen for every child. In our school systems, there's a belief teachers will provide ethical and moral lessons at school. This is quite different from merely *reinforcing* what has already been taught at home. When I was growing up, my parents taught me about honesty and cheating. Today, it is not unusual to catch children cheating. Sadly I hear them say they cheat because everyone else does. After talking with many teachers and coaches over the years, I hear a common thread about cheating. Students say they know cheating is wrong but they continue to do it anyway. It takes a seasoned teacher to get down all the tricks of the cheating trade. Just when you think you have it all figured out, students come up with more new and inventive methods of cheating. There is the classic cheat sheet stuffed up the sleeve, or the answers inside the lift-top desk or pencil box. Previously they may have written loads of information on their arm and wear a long-sleeve shirt to class. Don't underestimate the power of a rubber band. Stretch it out and you can get a lot of information written on that tiny piece of rubber. When they are done, and the rubber band is closed up, the answers disappear. An all time favorite is the urgent need for a student to go the bathroom in the middle of a test. Their Academy Award-winning performance of a distressed face is so convincing, I decide I better let them go. I'm certain they are going into the bathroom and pulling the answers from out their back pocket. What am I supposed to do? Strip search them before they leave? My remedy? I tell them to go to the bathroom before the test, as they will not be signing out until they are done. Plenty of discretion is involved in this decision, as I don't want to be mopping up barf in my classroom.

Cheating is prevalent on the written test. However, assessments can be done in a variety of other ways. This makes it harder for students to cheat. When projects are assigned, I tell them they'll be doing it in the classroom (You would not believe the parent relief I hear when I announce this during open house in September). There are four reasons for doing projects in school.

1. It prevents "others" from doing a student's project for them at home.
2. Doing the project at school allows me to see the process. What are they learning working step-by-step?
3. The result is important but the process is *more* important.
4. Doing the project in school forces students to take ownership of their project and understand the concepts behind them. This results in the students being able to carry on an intelligent conversation about their project rather than the usual, "This is my project. Now I will demonstrate it." I constantly emphasize the importance of a student knowing every aspect of their project.

The pressure to do well for many students can be overwhelming. Trying to find the balance between academics and after-school programs sometimes leads to drastic measures. Like cheating. A few students I interviewed said cheating is rampant. David believes kids today cheat because they are lazy, or there is too much pressure from parents for kids to succeed. I can remember telling my own kids if they don't try harder, they will be going to The University of Pepperell (my home town with absolutely no university). Sara says many kids believe everyone does it, so what is the big deal? Students copy papers from other students from the year before. Adrienne mentioned she did so poorly in a class because of poor teaching so she cheated on a test. To her, it was worth it to cheat rather than repeating the class. Miranda told me she was convinced she wasn't smart enough to earn a passing grade, so desperate times called for desperate measures. Emily was upset because she was in a class without her friends. The result was she didn't want to learn, so she cheated. Nikki thought it was pointless to memorize tons of formulas because the essential part of learning math was whether you knew the process and not memorizing a million formulas. To bypass that, she put the formulas on her calculator.

Final exams in high school can be tough for kids. Teaching all year and then asking students to recall all the information since September can be daunting for many students. Many of them find it a pressure situation and will resort to cheating tactics to pass the exam. I was teaching math in high school and preparing my students for the final exam. This one boy, Curtis, was doing very poorly and he needed a 90% on the exam to pass for the year. I was worried about his efforts as he didn't seem particularly motivated. Exam week came and he showed up the day of the test. He spent an hour in the room, placed the exam in the bucket, smiled and waved goodbye as he left. At the end of the day, I grabbed all the tests and went home. Being the end of the year, there was a time crunch to get the tests corrected and the grades done. So I'm going through the stack and I get to Curtis's test. Sadly, I see he has not studied at all as my red pen is making "x" marks one after another. Flipping to the last page, I see a staple in the top left hand corner. Turning the page over to see why, there staring me in the face is a green mug shot of Ulysses S. Grant. I can't believe it. I yelled to my husband, "I'm being bribed." I crack up laughing. Never before has *that* happened to me. Obviously Curtis wanted me to pass him on the exam in exchange for the fifty bucks. It took me awhile to figure out how I wanted to handle it. I corrected his test and he received an impressive 22% out of 100. Ahem! Not enough to pass the course. The next day Curtis came to my room to see if I had "corrected" his exam. "Yes, I have Curtis. Here you go." Curtis looked at the test, the grade and then looked at me, shocked. "What happened?" he said. "It looks like you didn't do much studying for the test," I said. "No," he said. "That's not what I mean. What about the money?" "The money?" I queried. "What money?" His eyes looked like they were going to pop out of his head. "The money stapled to the back of the test," he shouted. "I have no idea what you're talking about," I calmly said. The look in his eyes now was murderous. I stepped back a bit. "Sorry Curtis but I have a class now. By the way, the principal is expecting you in his office so if you could stop there after leaving here that would be great."

Curtis glared at me for another ten seconds, turned, walked out slamming the door behind him. I have to admit I was shaking a little. What Curtis *didn't* know, waiting for him in the principal's office was the fifty dollar bill and his parents.

A middle school student told me that kids suspect teachers will never figure out they're cheating. And you know, sometimes we don't. I always told my kids the proof was in the pudding. If you cheat on your homework, then the day of the test will be your day of reckoning. On the first day I emphasize to the students their need to do their homework. It's not busy work. It simply reinforces what they are learning in class. Homework also helps to prepare them for tests. Another student told me kids offer their papers to their friends all the time. There are too many opportunities to cheat and it is tempting, particularly if your buddy is willing to compromise his hard work. Adrienne feels more emphasis on study skills and strategies for self-motivation would have been helpful. Perhaps that would help to cut down on the cheating. A student may think they are not hurting anyone by cheating. They may blame the teacher or think the class they are taking is worthless.

In the end, can you live with yourself if you cheat? The Mark Kula Center for Applied Ethics says, "What is needed is a larger, more integrative vision of community in higher education . . . a place where individuals accept their obligations to the group and where well-defined governance procedures guide behavior for the common good." If that sounds high-minded but abstract, schools can use several specific strategies to create a community with greater academic integrity. Most basically, they can have a clear policy on cheating, make sure the policy is discussed, and enforce its provisions. You have to establish from the beginning of the class that there is such a low tolerance for cheating that no one feels they have to cheat to stay even." I believe I have an obligation to my students to instill in them that cheating is morally wrong, and socially unacceptable.

I REMEMBER WHEN . . .

Students would get so mad when they studied stuff they didn't "need" to. Phew! Imagine that. Getting a little "extra" knowledge.

Jamal tried to forge his father's name (Julian) on a test that had a poor grade. He apparently was so engrossed in doing such a good job of making the signature look like his dad's, he forgot to write his father's name and signed it "Jamal."

I told my students that the tests I had corrected were so bad I decided to grade them on a curve. Kelly asked me, "Were you in a car or a bus when you did that?"

My students were being a bit noisy and I asked all of them to put their eyeballs up on me. Gregg leaped from his seat, came right up to me and placed two Halloween eyeball candies right in my lap.

How could I *not* laugh!

I received a note from a parent asking if I would be willing to come in to school on a Saturday to help their son with school work but only **IF** the Saturday was a rainy day. I had to call to see if this note was genuine.

It was.

In 2001 I jokingly told the class when they were doing their Civil War project they would receive extra credit if they had someone come to class and speak about their experiences in the Civil War. After a few seconds, Linda slammed her hand down on the desk exclaiming that was totally unfair because all of her family came from California. She actually ran out of the room crying.

CHAPTER NINE

YOU MEAN I'M NOT FIRED?

"I've come to the frightening conclusion that I am the decisive element in the classroom. It's my daily mood that makes the weather. As a teacher, I possess a tremendous power to make a child's life miserable or joyous. I can be a tool of torture or an instrument of inspiration. I can humiliate or humor, hurt or heal. In all situations, it is my response that decides whether a crisis will be escalated or de-escalated and a child humanized or de-humanized."—Dr. Haim Ginott

It's the responsibility of a teacher to create a safe environment in the classroom so children can attempt to answer questions and take risks—even when they're wrong. This fosters a climate of students working together and not competing against each other. It helps students to be more courageous. Teachers seem to be more sensitive about this issue than in years gone by. I can remember during gym classes when the teacher would line us up against the wall and then pick two captains to choose the teams. Guess what happens. The kids who are the super athletes got chosen first. Eventually the crowd whittles down to the remaining few that *nobody* wants on their team. Who's the best of the worst? It's terribly humiliating. I think those days are behind us. But students who constantly have a feeling of inadequacy are still with us today.

But what about teachers taking risks? Just as I am obligated to make students feel comfortable, what about administrators making the teachers feel safe in the classroom. I can remember working in a school that required me to fill out my lesson plan books a week in advance. It was difficult to be that specific a week ahead of time. During the day while I was teaching, the plan book was to remain open on my desk in the event a principal or superintendent would cruise through the building. If they came into my room, I was supposed to be teaching *exactly* what was written in the plan box for that day. I hated it. Having this pressure to conform to their rules never allowed me to go outside the box. If I changed the lesson plan earlier in the morning, I had to erase everything in the box and rewrite my plans for the day. I can't think of a better way to stifle a teacher than this. I lasted one year at that school. I am a risk taker. Being in the classroom *can* be structured and often times I wondered if I was boring the kids half to death or if my curriculum should be spiced up. My philosophy was, nothing ventured, nothing gained. Here are a few stories that demonstrate my risk-taking which have left a mark, literally and figuratively.

I had been doing a unit on chemistry and for an opener I wanted to show the students how sodium reacts with water. Sodium is a highly reactive alkaline metal that is silver in color when you open the package and then tarnishes when exposed to air. When they package sodium, it comes in a box, which is in a box, which is in another box surrounded by cat litter. The sodium pieces are in a container that has some sort of inert liquid to keep the pieces from reacting. I explained to the class that sodium is essential for all animals and for some plants. Most of the students recognized sodium as one of the elements in table salt. After opening all the boxes to get to the sodium, I was shocked to see the pieces in the container were so small. "I paid how much for these little tiny pieces of metal?"

To begin the class, I had a 1000mL beaker of cool water sitting on my front lab table. I told the students I would be dropping a small piece of sodium into the beaker. I had them hypothesize about the reaction they might see after dropping in the sodium. I should point out, I had never done this experiment before. I recall a story in the news a few years ago about some sodium found in the Charles River in Boston. On Sept. 6, 2007 a block of sodium was recovered by a volunteer crew working on a boat. The volunteers, who were working on the Boston side of the Charles River near Gloucester Street, picked the sodium up and placed it in a trash container along with other wet debris. The sodium caught fire and exploded, burning two volunteers and three paramedics who responded to the scene. I felt a little nervous about working with the sodium. But remember I told you, I was a risk taker. What was the worst that could happen?

I dropped the piece of sodium in the beaker and for a minute it skirted around the top, giving off a bright flash. Then it sputtered out. The students and I were a bit disappointed in the reaction. One of my students suggested we drop the sodium into warm water. I sent someone over to the sink to fill up the beaker with warm water. I guess it was my mistake to not clarify the definition of "warm." According to kids, there are various interpretations of warm. We all held our breath and waited as I dropped another piece of sodium into the beaker. The sodium took off in the beaker like a horse out of the starting gate. It flew around and around the top of the beaker about five times. Suddenly it burst into flames and a popping sound as pieces of sodium shot straight up to the ceiling. You should have seen the looks on the kid's faces, not to mention the shock and surprise on my face. There were collective gasps, screams, and peals of laughter erupting from around the room. The ceiling was peppered with tiny holes. I had visions of small fires igniting above the tiles and burning down the entire school. Safety is my number one concern and quickly I assessed the group of kids. Everybody seemed fine. I didn't blind or maim anyone. Of course, everyone wanted me to do it again. I decided not to push my luck. The students never forgot the power of sodium. Neither did I. By the way, please don't try this experiment at home.

* * *

As I mentioned before, always expect the unexpected when you're teaching. Perhaps there should be a clause in my contract that exempts me from being responsible for science experiments that go crazy. The lesson for today? To extract deoxyribonucleic acid (DNA for short) from spinach. DNA is the genetic coding that decides whether you are male or female, among other traits. In order to obtain DNA from spinach, you need to combine spinach, rubbing alcohol, dishwashing soap, meat tenderizer, water and salt. Throw all of this into a blender until you have a soupy mixture. After three minutes or so, turn off your blender and you will notice a white substance forming that looks similar to a cobweb. Simply take a glass stirring rod and twist it right off the top of the spinach glop. The DNA comes out in long, stringy shapes. Pretty cool.

I was teaching in a school where no science lab existed. The students' desks sufficed as lab tables. I set up five different stations in the room and each of them had a food blender. After explaining the procedure, the students went at it. At one particular station, the blender was having some trouble mixing the ingredients. The students kept taking the lid off to stir what was inside. When kids are working together and having a good time, sometimes communication can go awry. That being the case, what happened next was inevitable. While one student was taking the lid off to check the gloppy mixture, their partner turned on the blender. When I heard the yelp, I glanced over, just in time to see spinach flying up to the ceiling and landing in splotches all over the place. What a mess! Spinach was dripping from the ceiling and covering desks, students, and the carpet. Of course we erupted in laughter. Quickly we cleaned everything up but couldn't get to the ceiling. They were much too high. The spinach remains there as of today. Along with the blood stains (really red food coloring) from Rob's demonstration of the circulatory system that went haywire.

* * *

Computers and I have never been best friends. When they made their entrance into the world, I ignored them. When I had no choice, I made little effort to understand them. Back in the early 90s, I made my students hand-write any research paper I assigned (They could use the ever popular typewriter if they chose). The average student could write about a hundred words on a piece of lined paper. Around 1994, we had just put computers in the school and some students had computers at home. In most cases, it was students who had older siblings in high schools. Computer-typed papers were starting to be required. I had assigned a ten-page research paper to my middle school kids. One of my students asked me if they could type their paper on the computer. "Sure," I said. "No problem." He asked what size font he should use. He may as well have been speaking in a foreign language at that point. I can remember trying to sound educated and telling him, "Just type the words big enough so I can see them."

The next morning, after getting to school, I was summoned to the office. In the lobby was a very irate parent. She wanted to speak to me regarding the research paper. Before I could even ask what the problem was, she launched into this tirade about me assigning a 2500 word research paper. "This is outrageous," she cried. She expounded on the fact that just because I *used* to teach high school, I needed to understand these kids were just eighth graders who could not possibly handle that kind of assignment. I was so stunned I couldn't respond for a minute. My head was whirling trying to make sense of her anger. Then I realized my mistake when assigning the paper. It had been customary to assign research papers by the *number of pages* and *not the number of words*. I was completely clueless as to how many words could be typed on a page using a computer. Once she was done venting I replied, "I can completely understand why you are upset. This was a huge oversight on my part." I continued explaining how I had made this error. After a few minutes she was mollified. As she left the building, I could see my principal watching this exchange from a few yards down the hall. When she walked away, she was shaking her head. I wondered if it was for me or the parent. I did learn a valuable lesson. Do your research!

* * *

Earlier I had mentioned that after I was married we moved to Vermont and I replaced a teacher who suddenly left the school system. In addition to teaching physical education, I was also the field hockey coach. I was extremely nervous about taking over a varsity team in the middle of the season. The night before my first practice I played the "what if" game in my head over and over. What if the kids were too upset their old coach was being replaced? What if they wouldn't put out any effort because of a new coach? What if I was not hard enough or challenging enough as a coach? My fears were quickly put to rest as I integrated myself into the position. The players responded to me seamlessly. They were a wonderful group of students who were serious about their team, their skills, and were totally committed to continuing the season with hopes of making the playoffs.

After a week of practicing and coaching two away games, we had a home game that was making me somewhat nervous. It was our first home game since taking over the position. I was concerned about making a good impression on the parents. After warming up, I called the players in and assigned the starting lineup. Eleven girls ran onto the field and went to their various positions. The game ball was placed in the center, and referees called to each goalie to see if they were ready. Just as the game was about to start, the referee blew her whistle. She was about ten feet from me when she announced in a loud voice that the game could not start because my players had illegal field hockey sticks. "Illegal sticks? What's that all about?" I panicked, thinking I hadn't read the rulebook and was allowing my girls to play with sticks that were not regulation. How could I be so stupid? I looked out on the field and saw many of my girls were laughing. Thinking this was not funny at all, and downright embarrassing, I called them all in. They came running to me, huddled around and I said, "What's going on with the sticks? Let me see them." Slowly, one by one, each presented their sticks to me. To my shock, horror, and complete embarrassment, I saw every girl's stick on the field was covered with a condom. I was speechless. Turning around, I grabbed the nearest backpack sitting on the ground and simply said, "Put them in here, **NOW**." I didn't dare turn around and look at one parent. I thought my job was going disappear as quickly as it came. Apparently this was some sort of initiation rite for the "new" coach. In the end we all got a chuckle out of this incident but there was another valuable lesson learned here: check all equipment before starting a game

* * *

Teaching science involves labs and experiments with numerous amounts of materials. Cleanup is always the bane of every science teacher. The school I was teaching at one year was an old building. On the top floor was a storage closet just down the hall from my classroom. For some reason, there was a sink installed in there. This made it easy to access water for labs and cleanup as the bathrooms were located in the basement of the school. In this particular incident, I was teaching an earth science lab. Earth science has never been one of my favorite areas but I was required to teach it for an entire year. Much of my prep time was spent looking for quality activities and labs for earth science. This particular lab I chose required the students to bring in sand, small pebbles and a few medium size rocks. After spending a few days of working on this lab, it was time to throw away the sand and rocks. Somehow my announcement to the students about taking the stuff *outside* got lost in translation. Unbeknownst to me, a few kids took off down to the storage closet and deposited their buckets of sand and stones in the sink. When I noticed a few students missing and asked the class where they had gone, the kids told me they had gone into the storage closet to throw their stuff away. I panicked and rushed down there. "Don't put your stuff in the sink," I shouted. Too late. Desperately I began trying to dig out the rocks that were starting to clog the sink. Back in the classroom (which is obviously not being supervised) some kids thought it might be a good idea to throw their stuff out the window. Again, did *anybody* hear my announcement we would be throwing this stuff outside?

My windows had no screens. The kids just threw up the sash and a few pounds of sand and rocks went sailing out. The teacher who was in the room underneath me suddenly heard a thud outside her window. Because the deposits dropped so fast it was not clear as to *WHAT* was coming out the window. The distressed teacher thought an eighth grader had just fallen out the window. He went flying to the front office to report a falling body.

The principal comes racing upstairs to see what is going on. Of course I am *not* there. Great. I have left a room full of kids unsupervised. Totally unacceptable according the teachers handbook. That will impress the principal. Where am I? Still in the storage closet frantically trying to get the stones out of the drain. The sink was severely clogged at this point. A student came racing down to tell me the principal is in the room. "Peachy." I don't even want to go back there. But I knew I had to face the music. I assured the principal no eighth grader had fallen out the window. She was not too happy with me. The custodians even less so as they spent a long time fixing the sink. Even though I thought that might have been my last year there, they did let me come back!

* * *

Teaching chemistry is part of physical science. We do chemistry the last half of the year because everyone looks forward to it. I love seeing elements interact and hypothesizing about the outcomes of experiments. There is always an element of surprise when using hazardous chemicals and Bunsen burners. An exciting experiment demonstrating the definition of chemical changes requires yards of magnesium ribbon. Magnesium is an alkaline earth metal found at number 12 on the periodic table of elements. Magnesium is quite light; lighter than aluminum but very strong. In its raw form, it is silvery-white. Magnesium is used in the design of fireworks and was used in flash photography. It's also sold to science teachers like me who can purchase magnesium in long strips or ribbons. It would be difficult to light magnesium if you had it in mass quantities. And it would be very dangerous.

To begin, each child was issued a piece of magnesium ribbon. I had cut each piece about six inches long. Prior to starting the lab we discussed what chemical changes were and how lighting these strips was going to demonstrate those changes. Very thoroughly, I had gone over safety procedures with burning magnesium ribbon. Magnesium ignites quickly and burns with a white flame. It's quite spectacular. Looking at the flame closely and directly can injure your eyes. This seems like a risky experiment just to demonstrate chemical changes, but the strip burns so fast there is minimal danger to the student. Without any element of danger, would there be any fun? Every day I have at least one student who comes into class and asks, "Mrs. Fillip, can we blow something up today?" So, in a sense, today we were going to blow something up.

I was going to be burning magnesium ribbon in all five of my classes. Every class went off without a hitch. Well, almost. All the students safely and correctly burned their ribbons. Nothing gives me more satisfaction than the sounds of excitement when doing a lab with my kids. Eventually the room became smoky. I opened the windows to let the draft pull out the smoke. That worked and everyone was breathing fine. During the last class of the afternoon, the students had just finished their round of burning the magnesium. Because it was the last class, I had extra ribbon on my reel and decided the last class might as well use it all up. The kids were thrilled. I cut the remaining ribbon into equal strips so every student could have one more piece. The room was still a bit smoky from the first round but I had the windows open. I thought doing a second round would not be a problem.

They all lit the magnesium ribbon and gleefully watched their ribbon burn down. The room was quite smoky but everyone was breathing fine. Right after the ribbons had been extinguished, I had a student who came up to me and wanted some water from the fountain in the hallway. Not one to compromise safety for any student, I thought I should let him go as maybe the smoke had bothered him. As he went out the door, three things happened: (1.) The announcements for the end of the day had just come on; (2.) The student going out the door for water pushed the door hard enough to keep it open; and (3.) The draft from the opened door pulled all the smoke into the hallway.

Brrring went the fire alarm. I heard the principal shout over the PA, "I guess we'll be going outside now." As we filed out I could hear laughter and teachers calling out to me, "What did you do this time?" I guess my reputation preceded me. In a few minutes, the firemen and trucks roared into the school parking lot. I humbly had to explain it was indeed my fault. The firemen checked out the room and saw no fire, just lots of smoke. Because of the evacuation of the building, I managed to delay the busses and cause mass confusion with students who were not allowed back in the classroom to get their stuff. What was the lesson learned here? Know where your smoke alarm is located at all times. Incidentally, I seem to have a penchant for setting off fire alarms. Recently I set off the fire alarm at the Senior Citizen Center while carrying a birthday cake for my art teacher. The cake was full of lit candles. He was turning 93. As I brought it into the art room, I set it down on the table under the smoke alarm (In my defense I didn't know the alarm was there) and our teacher blew out the candles. *Brring!* In case you're wondering . . . yes, my house is still standing.

I REMEMBER WHEN...

From time to time, I would assign extra credit. It always seems to be the case that the kids who *don't* need extra points do the assignment and the kids who *do* need extra points take the work but then never seem to hand it in. It's really a no-brainer why this happens but I do think it's peculiar.

Marissa asked me if lunar moths were here today because the men brought them back after the first time they went to the moon.

Jill asked me if the world was round, why didn't the oceans always run downhill.

Danny thought cloning was taking a sheep and turning into a woman because, "the sheep's name was Dolly, which is a woman's name," he said.

The custodian in our school was a great guy but a tough old bird. Very manly and could handle anything you threw at him. His wife had succumbed to cancer and the funeral was held in the church next door to the school. The entire school was able to attend. It was very sad, but what tore at everyone's heart happened near the end of the funeral. This tough, stoic, guy was walking down the aisle with tears *pouring down his face* and his head was slightly tilted downward as the strains of "On Eagles Wings" poured from the organ. I doubt there was a dry eye in the church. You could feel the love, comfort, and prayers reaching out to him from the congregation. It was very special.

CHAPTER TEN

Teacher Anxiety

"The secret of teaching is to appear to have known all your life what you learned this afternoon."—Anonymous

How many of you have ever experienced "going back to school anxiety?" I believe it's a real problem. No matter how many years I have taught, the night before the first day of school in September *never* allows me a good night's sleep. I have spoken to many teachers about this. We actually joke about the first day being exhausting because of first-day eve jitters. It's not that I am worried I will do poorly or make a bad impression on the kids. It's difficult to explain if you have not experienced this. An analogy might be the first time you ever flew in an airplane. Nervous but excited. The anxiety is combined with excitement, expectation, and unanticipated moments. To meet a new group of students for the year impacts me the same way I impact the student. In other words, we are sizing each other up.

But back-to-school anxiety happens more often than just at the beginning of a new school year. Lynnette mentioned to me she has anxiety every Sunday night. For some reason, she starts getting anxious Sunday evening and sometimes it's so bad, she calls in sick for Monday. The closing days of a school vacation seems to be even worse. She said emotionally she hopes the vacation will go on for a few more days despite being prepared for class. "I can't describe the feeling," she said. "It's almost a panic feeling." Realistically, Lynnette is aware she has to go back to school. But she can't seem to get her brain wrapped around the idea. The thought of going to school and performing adequately might lead to some teaching anxiety. No one wants to fail. Teachers want to believe they can help each student reach his or her potential. Facing a classroom of eager and expectant faces as a new teacher can be quite daunting. Dealing with parents can be even scarier, especially when you're new.

The first year I taught high school biology, I was nervous about knowing the subject well enough to teach it. Was I really qualified? My teaching certificate *said* I was, but what about all those geniuses in the room who might get bored with me, find the curriculum unchallenging, or worse, ask me questions I cannot answer. When I started teaching, it seemed scary to be unprepared or not know something. I kept comparing myself to other teachers. They seemed so much more intelligent than I. In biology class I was teaching a lesson on the three states of matter (back in the late 70s) and had read *somewhere* that a fourth state of matter had been discovered. I told the class that plasma was then considered a fourth state of matter. Alan, the smartest kid in the class, raised his hand and asked, "What is it?" I had no idea. But it sounded intelligent. I knew plasma was found in our bodies and happened to mention that. Alan looked at me as if I was crazy. "What has that got to do with states of matter?" he asked. My face burned, I was totally humiliated. I thought, "Why did I ever *bring that up*?" Quickly, I shifted gears and began another topic. No way was I going to show my ignorance. I learned a very valuable lesson that day. Don't present information unless you really know what you're talking about. It's acceptable to say, "I don't know but I will find out." I felt like I had lost a little credibility that day. Teachers are not expected to have all the answers or know about *everything*. Students are smart, critical thinkers and can put you on the spot if you're not prepared.

* * *

Coaching varsity field hockey resulted in an interesting intervention from a parent. Tryouts brought 31 girls to my field and my goal was to select 16 to 17 girls for varsity. A field hockey team hosts 11 players on the field at a time. After three days of drills and skills workouts, I knew who I would select for the team. When I began to write down the names of the girls I chose, an amazing phenomenon occurred. Of the 17 girls on the team, seven of them were named Jenny! There was also a Jacqueline, Joan, Jillian, Julianne, Jessica, Jocelyn and Jody. Out of 17 girls, 14 of them all began with the letter "J." Oh my goodness! Surely I would be tripping over my tongue with all those J names. But how was I ever going to manage seven Jennys? Soliciting ideas from the girls, they came up with a plan in which each Jenny would be assigned a number. Something like Jenny McDonald was "one" and Jenny Groshman was "two" and so on and so forth. The team and I agreed to memorize them this way and the Jennys agreed to call themselves by their respective numbers. It was the only solution we had. The number system seemed to work out pretty well until the day of the first game.

Playing our first home game, I put five Jennys out on the field to start. As the game progressed, I did my usual antics and sideline coaching to motivate my players. The first time I called for a substitute from the bench, I told Jessica to go in for number five. Both Jessica and I knew that number five was "Jenny five." As Jessica ran onto the field, the scorekeeper from the other team flipped out. "I thought your player was going in for number five?" she shouted over to me. "She did," I shouted back. "Then why is number 18 coming off the field," the scorekeeper yelled back. My first thought was, "What's her problem?" Then I suddenly realized what she was getting at. We had named all the Jennys by numbers but they did *not* match the numbers on their shirts. Big problem. I couldn't change the Jenny number situation until after the game was over. I continued with our original plan. Behind me I could hear the parents asking, "What's the deal with the numbers?" After a period of time, I turned to Jenny number seven and said, "Seven! Go in for number one." Jenny seven leaped up and ran in to replace Jenny one.

While I was cleaning up from the game, I noticed Jenny seven and her parents hovering nearby. It didn't appear as though they were ready to leave. In fact, it looked like they wanted to talk to me! I approached them and asked if there was something they had a concern about. Jenny seven's dad was particularly provoked. My heart started to beat faster. I could feel the anxiety in the pit of my stomach and noticed my cold, clammy hands. A dreaded parent encounter! He raised his voice and told me it was pathetic how I numbered the girls instead of calling them by their names. He said it was degrading and humiliating. I tried to explain the reason why the team came up with this plan but he would not hear any of it. After a few futile attempts, I gave up. As he was leaving, he told me if I was going to call his daughter by a number, then it better be *number one*. He and his wife stalked off. His daughter turned to me and mouthed, "Sorry." I stood there dumbstruck and humiliated. Immediately I began to cry and decided I was not cut out for teaching or dealing with parents. No one during my student teaching prepared me for that. Thirty-four years later, I recall that incident with amusement. But it takes time and experience to build the armor necessary for teaching.

I REMEMBER WHEN . . .

One of my gymnasts knocked me out while I was trying to spot her on the uneven bars. She spent the rest of the season apologizing.

A student put a rubber spider in my desk drawer and truly I thought it was real. I screamed so loud it brought three teachers to my rescue.

I was showing a slide show of optical illusions on my own carousel and apparently had missed taking out a slide of my son stark naked when he was about two years old.

We went to a basketball game and the opposing coach came up to one of my players, shaking her hand, welcoming her to the gym and telling her that "her team" could use the locker room now and there would be a brief coaches meeting with the referees in a few minutes. She completely ignored me. and then on the *other* hand . . . .

I dressed up as a nun for Halloween at school. The irony is everyone knew I was a Mormon. A woman came into the school not aware we had been dressing up for Halloween. She spied me to get directions for somewhere in the building. Apparently I must have looked "old." "Excuse me," she started. "Are you the Mother Superior?"

CHAPTER ELEVEN

Role Reversal

"Thoroughly to teach another is the best way to learn for yourself."
—*Tyron Edwards*

    Todd came flying into class one day waving a magazine. "Mrs. Fillip, I found this cool article in a magazine on how bouncy balls are made. Can you look at it? Do you think we can make these in class?" I told him to put the magazine on my desk and I would look at it later. I wasn't putting Todd off. I *would* look at it later.
    This kind of thing happens all the time. Sometimes students will share information in class that is new to me. I might stop the class, take a minute and look it up on the Internet to check for accuracy. Frequently I am encouraging this. I always tell my students to think of ways to extend their labs we have done. On their lab reports, they are required to come up with a question that would further test their objective. For example, we were doing a lab on harnessing carbon dioxide using items like soda pop and elodea. Yvette asked me if there was a way to measure the amount of carbon dioxide released when eating Pop Rocks candy. We figured out a way to test it. The student who suggested it beamed. Using ideas from kids is definitely a motivator for them to be more creative. All students love to hear a teacher tell the class where the new information came from. In the past, I always felt intimidated when students told me something I didn't know. My first thought was, "How come I don't know that!" Eventually I realized I didn't have to feel threatened. My role as a teacher was to maintain a flexible and open attitude. This encourages students to increase their problem solving skills. I grew up in an era where it was forbidden to correct the teacher or

challenge them with new ideas. There were serious consequences if you even tried. My philosophy is to foster an environment in the classroom that allows me to be a supporter and facilitator. Each year my comfort zone widened as I allowed students to express their ideas.

Whether in the United States or Australia, high school kids are getting turned off to computer technology because they often know more than their teacher. It's a serious issue. The problem is society, including educators, tends to focus more on the technology and less on how these tools get people to think and interact. Part of me is glad I don't teach high school any longer just because of the sophistication of today's technology. I don't *however*, believe students in the younger grades feel this way. They still look to the teachers for guidance and help.

Kids jumped at the chance to come over to my computer when I would shout, "Help!" It would have been technological suicide for me had I not asked. The students were miles ahead of me with their knowledge. In 2007, the idea of *teaching* from a PowerPoint was just merely a blip on the horizon for me. And who has the time to learn such things? At the time, I had a group of seventh graders with one or two students who knew how to put together a PowerPoint presentation. I felt compelled to have my students use computers more often but definitely lacked the expertise needed to complete quality projects based on computer skills. I thought about taking some lessons from the computer gurus who worked in the school building. Should that be mandatory training for teachers? Then it dawned on me I could learn to make a PowerPoint using my own students. The PowerPoint is such a useful tool for teaching and sharing knowledge. This technique also saves countless hours of writing notes on the board.

Historically, the first version of the PowerPoint was called the Presenter. It was developed by Bob Gaskins and Dennis Austin. The name was changed to PowerPoint and bought out by Microsoft in 1987. The first version was released in 1990 by Microsoft 3.0. The software became popular and eventually specialized projection equipment grew up alongside it. PowerPoint has never had any serious competition. Today over 40 million use this amazing tool.

How was I going to learn the skills needed to make a PowerPoint and assign a project with specific criteria? The first step required was to come up with an idea for a project. I was thinking how insular kid's lives are. I couldn't take them on a field trip around the world, so why not bring the world to the classroom. I put together a portfolio with pictures and descriptions of over 200 natural wonders of the world. Students had time to browse through the portfolio and pick out a natural wonder for a PowerPoint presentation. I emphasized how they should pick a place they didn't know anything about. I wanted the students to learn something. My goal was to see 75 different presentations. I didn't want any duplicates. Basically every student got to choose the natural wonder they wanted. I picked one myself. The students were nervous because 99 %t of them were unfamiliar with the skills needed to make a PowerPoint. "Don't worry," I told the class. "I have absolutely no clue how to make one either." My confession seemed to calm down many students. I'm sure they were thinking, "If the teacher doesn't even know what she is doing, she can't get mad at us if we totally screw up."

We began working on our PowerPoint presentations in the computer room. The teacher's computer had the ability to project my work up on a large screen. The two PowerPoint whiz kids in the class were our teachers and began tutoring us. They were working on their own computers and dictated to me what I should do. As I began constructing my slide show, the display screen allowed the entire class to see the process. Slowly, class by class, we all accomplished the intricacies of designing a PowerPoint. Of course the students caught on much quicker than I did! It was heartwarming to see students helping other students and thrilling for students to teach something to a teacher. Many of them got a kick out of that.

The natural wonder presentation projects consisted of ten slides. My rubric set the criteria for each slide but I was looking for creativity and originality. Deadline day arrived and it was time to present the PowerPoints. This was another learning curve for me as well as the students. Since I had never used a PowerPoint to teach, I couldn't offer any great advice on how to present using one. I could only use my knowledge from previously *viewing* a power point done by another professional. I put my PowerPoint up first and went through the 10 slides. Every student was required to critique my presentation based on two parts: the content of the slides and how well I presented. While I was presenting, I reminded myself I was setting the tone for what I wanted my students to do. While the kids were critiquing me, I reminded them to be honest. "Don't be afraid to give me constructive criticism. It *won't* affect *your* grade." Again, the kids were having such a thrill grading the teacher. When I was done presenting, I collected their critiques and went over them with the class. The strategy was to help all of them feel more comfortable and better prepare them for their presentations. I wanted the students to critique each other, a valuable tool in education. Students become much more invested in the entire project this way. It can instill a sense of pride in what they've done. They believe their opinions are worthwhile.

The presentations were superb. I was pleasantly surprised, entertained, and enlightened by the effort from my students. Watching each child's project was akin to taking a mini trip around the world. I was astonished at how little I knew. There are so many fascinating places in the world. Aside from the top seven natural wonders of the world, we traveled to the Okavango Delta in Botswana, the Stone Forest in Yunnan Province, China, the Waitomo Caves in New Zealand, and the Giant's Causeway in Northern Ireland. There were dozens of other places, too many to mention.

My students and I felt such a sense of accomplishment. The PowerPoint became my friend. Suddenly I had to design a PowerPoint for everything I was teaching. It became addictive. Additional projects included man-made wonders of the world with a focus on physics, strange and unusual animals, our space program, catastrophic weather, and the list went on. Because I took a chance in requiring students do a project in which everyone needed to learn a skill, it opened up doors for everybody. I am grateful for my students being wonderful teachers.

What else have I learned from my students other than computer skills? Students have shown me not every child learns at the same rate or can adapt to every teaching style. Everyone is capable of learning but not everyone learns in the same way. Through the years, I have improved on my ability to teach with differentiated instruction. I have learned sensitivity, patience, empathy, and compassion. Not all children are fortunate to have idyllic lives. By admitting that I don't know everything, I have learned humility. Being with children all day allows me to know what tunes are popular, where you are supposed to put the newest piercing, and what sneakers are "in." I have learned kid lingo like "sick" means good. They have taught me that I need to keep learning just as they do. My kids have told me not to give up when I am trying to conquer something, like losing weight. Digging deeper gives the greater reward. I wouldn't be honest if I said I loved every child that came through my classes the past 34 years. But other students have shown me how to love even the worst student.

The teacher should know more than his or her students. But I have learned it's acceptable to ask for help from them. Whether I'm an expert, my goal for a student is to help them achieve his or her true potential. I've had pupils who are extremely intelligent and in those cases the role of the teacher should be a guide and facilitator more than a source of knowledge. The same thing goes for coaches. There are plenty of athletes who are more gifted at playing the sport than their own coach. There are some incredible coaches who were not incredible athletes. The coach is supposed to coach, not prove they are on par with their players. Some of my own coaches never played the sport but were dynamic in motivating me, increasing my skills, and inspring me to become a better person. One spring, the high school in Vermont where I was employed was desperate for a softball coach. I just completed two seasons of coaching and was looking forward to a break. The athletic director (AD) hounded me for a couple of days to take the job. I kept telling him I was not a softballplayer, barely knew the sport, and really was not a good candidate for the position. The AD insisted those things weren't important. "Nancy," he said. "You are already a coach. You know how to motivate and inspire. Conditioning is the same as all the other sports. Just read the rule book and the kids will take care of the rest. Please? We are desperate." I caved in because I felt bad for the girls. Most of the girls were my field hockey players so they were delighted to have me. I am a lousy softball player. I can't thow a ball to save my life. But my athletic director was right. I was there to coach them, not be a player. I conditoned them, kept the practices going, read the rule book, and the girls did take care of the rest. Of course at the first game I had a girl "slide" into first base and my husband sidled up to me and whisper in my ear that it was okay to over run first base. I didn't teach her that. Really!

The idea of being a better coach even if you are not a gifted athlete reminds me of the time I went to summer gymnastics camp at age 34. At the time I was coaching a varsity level gymnastics team in my high school. We had a very talented team. In the fall, an Olympic-level gymnast was going to join our team. I was so excited but nervous about my ability to work with her. I wasn't confident I could spot her on difficult moves or teach her how to improve. She was beyond any gymnast I have ever coached, not to mention her ability to perform moves I never learned in college. I thought the only way I could really understand her ability and help her was to go to a gymnastic camp and be a gymnast myself. The camp I chose was in New York and upon arriving I found I was was the oldest enrollee. Most of the kids thought I was a coach. Compared to the other kids, I looked like a blimp but in reality I was still pretty small. Being blonde, I looked years younger than I was. The coaches thought I was in high school.

On the first day of camp, we worked out two hours in the morning, three hours in the afternoom, and two hours in the evening. I learned how to spot all kinds of gymnastic tricks. I participated as a gymnast and felt comfortable trying anything because they had these big, burly guys who would catch me if I fell. I collapsed into bed that night, utterly exhausted. When I woke up the next morning and stepped out of bed, every muscle in my entire body was screaming. Even my little toes hurt. I couldn't even move. Never, and I can say this without exaggerating, *never* have I been so sore from a physical workout. I could barely get dressed. Lifting my arms up to brush my hair was intolerable. I hobbled to the dining room for breakfast and reminded myself I was *not* a teenager. What was I thinking? Warming up in the gym an hour later was torture. I watched with admiration and envy as girls sat in mile wide straddles with their heads down on the mat. I couldn't do that *before* yesterday. The thought of stretching my hamstrings almost made me me cry. I couldn't even sit down without hurting. I spent most of the day watching coaches coach. I kept justifying it, telling myself that this was the main reason why I came there. I learned quite a bit. The next morning I was still as flexible as a piece of cement so I made the decision to go home. The pain and discomfort was preventing me from being a gymnast and I was tired of watching. One of the coaches told me it was probably for the best, as I was so "old." I drove the seven hours back home and realized my forte was in being a coach. I didn't have to keep up with the kids.

Teaching and coaching have taught me how to be human. Math was such a struggle for many kids and I told them I completely understood. My eighth-grade math teacher told me I was hopeless and don't ever think of becoming a math or science teacher. "Don't worry, I never will," I told her. But children will teach everyone not to underestimate the power of ambition. My students taught me not settle for mediocrity and to challenge them for greater rewards.

Letting kids give feedback on your teaching is a meaningful assessment of yourself. At the end of each semester, I make my own evaluation sheet for the kids. It allows them to critique projects, labs, demonstrations and activities as well as other teaching traits about me. I put a lot of stock in those critiques. After all, they are with me every day. Kids can be very candid and frank and I appreciate that. Appealing to students by providing an event (such as questions that evaluate their teacher) is an excellent way to begin the empowerment process. It is important to ask students for their opinions, hear what they say and accept it. I believe too often teachers reshape student responses into what they think students mean and this has the potential to devalue what they actually think. Students often feel they don't have a voice and are not really being listened to. Setting the ground rule under which everyone is equal and under which students are treated with respect is essential. Many a project has been filed under wastebasket because of the feedback I have received. Principals need to do an evaluation on all teachers. I value their feedback as well. But it doesn't feel as honest as when the kids evaluate me. A scheduled evaluation by a principal allows the teacher to prepare the best lesson they ever gave. A true evaluation would be a pop-in visit. Evaluations can be helpful but one of the best ways for teachers to improve is by observing other teachers. In my entire teaching career, I rarely did that. I found this well-suited quote. "I have taught 20,000 classes; I have been 'evaluated' thirty times; but I have never seen another teacher teach."

I know many of my students are far better at many things than I am. What they are *not* better at is teaching. I make it clear that I am very good at teaching what I teach. But I also make it clear it is no more possible to be first-rate at all kinds of science or math than to be as excellent in every language if you only speak French. I am well educated in each of the three areas of science; earth, life and physical. But I don't claim to know everything. My job is to teach science, but I believe I am armed with general knowledge of life outside the science arena. I usually have time to talk about interesting material not related to science because I have been living longer and had more experiences than the kids. These are powerful learning opportunities for them and the students enjoy these moments. During break times from the regular class, my students learn about all sorts of new and interesting venues. In addition, the kids seem to enjoy hearing about my frustrations, crazy or exciting stories, or how stupid it makes me feel when I can't learn something. I become more human. Every teacher should *have* to be a student and struggle so they can remember what it's like to be on the other side.

I had an opportunity to sample what it's like to be on the other side. In 2005 I suffered a brain injury. For years I had battled a vertigo problem that resulted in frequent falls, broken bones, trips to the hospital, and the ultimate—a brain injury. One day at school, I lost my balance and hit my head on the floor. I was hospitalized for six months, part of that time at Spaulding Rehabilitation Hospital in Boston. I was a patient on the eighth floor, which is for traumatic brain injuries. Why would I tell you this? Because despite everything I went through, it opened my eyes. A new perspective of how students learn was revealed to me. Because of the way I hit my head, I had bilateral paralysis. When I was sitting or lying down, I could move my legs. As soon as I stood up, there was no message from my brain to my legs to move and I was unable to walk. I was in a wheelchair for almost a year. Due to my lack of ability to get around, I was stunned at how inaccessible life was strapped in a wheelchair. Many establishments still do not have wheelchair access. More disconcerting was the sudden decrease in my cognitive ability to focus and remember. I couldn't watch TV because it was too difficult to follow. Reading was not an option because I couldn't stay with the story line. Even writing a letter was a significant challenge. My only entertainment was listening to music and visiting with friends. In addition, I had difficulties with my attention span. I was incredibly distracted while doing any task. The doctor told me I would never walk again or go back to teaching.

Many months later, the entire experience gave me tremendous insight for students who have learning disabilities. I have taught students in my class with learning disabilities or behavioral issues. I've read the paperwork and talked with the special education teachers to accommodate their needs. These specialists are in my classroom and I am grateful for their help. But I always felt I didn't quite understand the mechanics behind my students' struggles. Because of the brain injury, I feel I have walked in their footsteps somewhat. It took me a long time to get back to 100 percent. I couldn't concentrate on the smallest task. My attention span was shorter than a six-inch ruler. Forget about the memory. I couldn't multitask and was incredibly disorganized. Dyslexia was obvious. I can remember doing crossword puzzles with clues such as, "a three-letter word for a furry animal that says meow." When I was able to return to teaching (a year and half later) I had a new appreciation for kids who struggle with their schoolwork. My problems only lasted a few years. Some students struggle their whole lives. Now when I hear the frustrations of a child who can't understand, I remember where I've been. When I hear a struggling student say they are stupid, my heart goes out to them. I know exactly what they mean. For months I branded myself as stupid, while everyone on my medical team told me it would all pass. It is my job, as a teacher, no matter what level of ability a student has, to encourage them and get them to believe they can achieve anything they want. Yes, some have to work harder than others, but the potential is no different. It's all about choices. If you want to succeed, you will.

I REMEMBER WHEN . . .

I was reflecting that every day we all come together; teachers students, staff, and we all work for a common cause. Among us there is such diversity and yet, we are all the same. The same traits that make us human. We all smile in the same language; we all cry when we are sad, we comfort each other and reach out to help each other in times of need. It reminded me of this memory where diversity didn't matter. What mattered was that we were there for each other.

I had student who was an avid skier. He was also somewhat of a daredevil. Apparently he and his friend were at a local mountain in Vermont and near the end of the day decided to ski off the groomed path of a rather difficult trail. Their spontaneous decision proved to be fateful. My student lost control and slammed head first into a tree. He was not wearing a helmet. His friend skied for help and they got him to the hospital shortly. The first night in the hospital the doctors precluded he would not survive the night. The towns people heard the news and decided they needed to have a candle light prayer vigil in the town hall immediately. I'm not sure how that message got out, but by the time I got to the town hall there was literally not enough room to even squeeze in to the town hall it was so packed with people. So I stood outside all night with my candle next to strangers who were there for the same reason. To save this one teenager. People from the town hall came out periodically to replace the outside people so they could get warm. It was remarkable. Perfect strangers working together in perfect harmony all for the common good. I still marvel over that. The student made it through the night. I am convinced it was the strength and the power of prayer. He remained in a coma for four months. After coming out his coma, he made a full recovery. He eventually came back to school, finished the work he missed during the summer, and was able to start school in the fall with his regular class. It was a miracle. The whole time, nobody cared who anybody was, what ethnicity they were, what house they lived in, how much money they made, or what kind of car they drove. They just cared that this one boy would live through the night.

CHAPTER TWELVE

Connections

"We cannot always build the future for our youth, but we can build our youth for the future."—Franklin D. Roosevelt

The philosophy behind teachers and students integrating 180 days of the year requires they have a common goal. In all the schools I have taught in, the mission was the same. We must prepare students to leave school and be able to cope in real-life situations. Whether kids graduated from my class in 1976 or 2010, the most essential thing they could take with them is confidence, skills, and a strong sense of identity. The idea of having attributes to think, solve problems, and work collaboratively should be the task of every educator. Our world has so much diversity and we are connected to each other much closer than we realize. It's up to a teacher to personalize teaching so they can move students along with these goals in mind. The goal of the student should be to make connections to the outside world, be able to keep up with ever-changing technology, and be able to adapt to new insights and ideas.

One of the activities I used to do with my students was called "connections." Typically this was done in our advisory sessions. Advisory is a group of students and one teacher that meet every day for about 45 minutes with a specific activity in mind. The group stays the same for the entire year and it is up to the group to decide what they will do each day. The purpose of advisory is for the students to get to know one teacher very well should they need to talk to someone, and they form a small community within a larger one. Advisory is very empowering. I had the opportunity to practice this in another school where we did it twice a week for a shorter time period and we called it something different. But it still had the same impact. My kids loved it. The idea of connections allowed a student to share about themselves either simplistically or in depth. They could talk about what happened yesterday, today, and what might happen tomorrow. Students could talk about their joys, sorrows, fear, concerns or just tell about their pet hamster. There are no rules about what they can or cannot say. Prior to connections, there is a conversation about appropriateness and use of language. Students sit in a circle facing each other and one person talks at a time. They can share anything they want. They may talk as long as they want unless they seem to dominate the time. Then it's up to the facilitator to remind them they need to conclude. The rules are quite simple; a student does not have to speak but needs to be a listener, a person may only have one turn to speak in the time frame set for connections, listeners are *not* to respond back to the speaker verbally or with any body language that denotes a negative message. Essentially, this is not an open discussion.

How do students benefit from connections? During the 10-15 minutes of the group sharing, students don't initially realize they are building a bridge toward each other. The first day of connections can be torture. Imagine a group of students sitting down and facing each other, some of whom really don't know each other. I know for a fact kids are already in the process of sizing each other up, judging each other, and thinking about whether they like each other. Some have already made their decision. The idea of connections is to break down these preconceived ideas. While it is never expected these students will all become bosom buddies at the end of the year, some amazing transformations take place in regard to relationships.

That first day of connections is tough. After explaining the rules and the protocol we follow, I announce that connections are "open." Instantly I notice two things. The kids are either looking around at each other, or they have their eyes down. I see lots of squirming feet. Uncomfortable smiles are sliding up the sides of their mouths. No one wants to go first. No one really knows what to say or what's appropriate for connections. Many of them are thinking, "what if they laugh at me?" "What if they think what I am saying is stupid?" "Will they tell their other friends outside of this group what I said?" There is a moment of silence. Then thirty more seconds of more silence. Finally, a student who can't stand the silence will start to speak. She might talk briefly and say what she is doing this coming weekend. But it's enough to get the ball rolling. Soon more kids are talking. Then someone breaks protocol and responds to another student. I gently remind them this is not a discussion. Responding back does not give the listener time to reflect on what someone is saying. Usually near the end of the first connections about half the students have spoken. As you look around the circle and take note of the silent kids, you realize these are your quiet students in the classroom on a regular basis. That is okay.

As weeks go by, almost all of your students are now participating in connections. In fact, there are the students who want to talk more than once, who want to respond, or want to talk too long. This is a good thing. They are enthusiastic. But more importantly, students are starting to trust each other. They begin sharing more personal stories and feelings alongside their connections. As the kids hear each other, they realize that the boy or girl they never knew, who they thought was so different from them, really have much more in common. The trials and tribulations of these students begin to emerge and allow everyone to see a commonality among each other. I notice students talking with other students they used to ignore. There enters a sense of respect and civility in the room. Students become more compassionate and understanding of each other. The class seems calmer and students begin working collaboratively even when assigned a "dreaded" partner. I've had students tell me they love connections and wish they could do it every day. I recommend twice a week. Another student told me they were so glad we have connections because they know other students so much better and it widened their circle of friends.

How do I benefit from connections? First let me say: periodically I share in connections. After I share a feeling that is honest and open, it gives them confidence to do the same. By hearing from my students in this forum, I begin to understand them much better. Often times the behavior of students doesn't make sense. This can lead to frustration and impatience. Connections allow me to get on a more personal level with these kids. The better I know my students, the better I can serve them. Students will demonstrate certain behaviors that keep themselves protected. Connections help to break down those barriers by letting them be honest about themselves. I then see the students more humanly and can often resonate with their feelings.

When my dad died, I was completely devastated. Upon returning to school, I was having some trepidation about how I would feel in the classroom. More so, I was worried about how the kids were going to respond to me after being out for over a week. The kids rolled in on the first day back and there was some initial tension in the room. The students were not quite sure how to speak to me. It was awkward. I decided we should do connections on that first day. As we formed our circle, I could sense they were wondering what was going to happen. Being the facilitator, I explained the rules and then announced connections were open. There was dead silence. More seconds passed and nobody spoke. I think they were waiting for me to speak. Then I began. "I missed you all this past week. It was a tough week for me." Silence. Then a voice from the circle said, "Not as much as we missed you." Instantly I could feel the tears prick the back of my eyelids. And then the questions came pouring out of their mouths. "How did your dad die?" "Where is he buried?" "What was your favorite memory of him?"

As I responded to each of their questions, I began to relax. Suddenly the topic of losing someone became the theme. Kids started telling me about losing their dog, their grandma, their goldfish, and other personal things. It was a connection that lasted 30 minutes and nothing since has been more heartfelt. I felt a bridge was rebuilt and our little community inside the classroom was stronger than ever. I was so grateful for their candidness, honesty and curiosity. Moreover, I was grateful for their compassion, kindness, and caring that flowed around that circle. This is why I do connections.

I REMEMBER WHEN . . .

I had surgery and these were some comments on the cards that came from my seventh and eighth graders:

Hope you feel better. Love, Meredith,
your perfect angle in class

I was wondering since you like to dissections and stuff if when they take out your gaul bladder they can save it so we can see it here in class and we can dissect it some more and stuff. Mrs. Fillip, can you ask the docter please? I've never seen one. Jason

Please hurry back. The substitute is not crazy like you. Vivian

We miss you. Class is boring. We have to do real work like read out the book and stuff. Best regrads, Matt

I hope you are enjoying your stay. Must be nice. You don' have to make your bed, or cook your food, or clean your room. Hurry back from your vacation so you can get back to work and get back to reality. Lillie

Hope you get better quick. I think I behave better when you are here because you give me that look when I am about to do something I'm not suppose to. I got a detention already so come back soon please. Thank you. Ike

Cuz you're a science teacher see if you can get some free stuff for the classroom like hearts while your there ok? Oh ya, hope your stomach is ok so you can eat your favorite—donuts hahahahah bye Jeremy

CHAPTER THIRTEEN

Drama Queen

"Good teaching is one-fourth preparation and three-fourths theater."
—Gail Goodwin

Sometimes I think I should have majored in theater. I love a captive audience. And what better audience could I have than a group of middle school students, particularly when we are doing chemistry. Kids are fascinated with reactions, fire, and explosions. Many chemistry experiments result in a "wow" factor when you involve hazardous materials. One of my science books talked about mixing sulfuric acid and sucrose together in equal amounts to create an amazing phenomenon. It seemed like a fun opener for class. Before I began, I wanted to make sure there was proper ventilation. Behind my science lab was a regular classroom that had a row of windows arrayed on one side of the wall. It seemed like a good place to do the experiment. I brought my students in the room and gathered them in a semicircle about three feet from one of the open windows. We had a brief discussion about sucrose and sulfuric acid. I didn't want to give too much away and spoil the surprise. I placed the empty beaker right up next to the screen. In their notebooks my students hypothesized about the outcome of combining clear sulfuric acid and white sucrose. When I was ready to perform the experiment, I had them don their safety glasses.

First I put the sucrose in the beaker. Then I added the sulfuric acid. This is the "AAA" rule. **ALWAYS ADD ACID.** In other words, always *add* an acid to any other chemicals as opposed to the other way around. This is a cardinal rule in chemistry. Quickly I stirred and stepped back to let everyone see. Within a few seconds, the mixture began to move slowly, back and forth, like a lazy wave. It was beginning to give off a vapor. I put my hands around the beaker and could feel the warmth. Combined, the two substances were still white in color. Suddenly, the mixture began to bubble, gurgle, and visibly change from white to a light brown, then almost black. I heard the "oohs" and "aaahs" and felt the anticipation of the students waiting for the grand conclusion. The mixture in the beaker began to rise higher and higher, creating a column. The black mass retained the shape of the beaker as it rose. The higher the mixture rose, the blacker it became. I tried to hold the beaker but it became too hot to touch. The stench of the vapors started to infiltrate the room. Within minutes, I realized the open window was not doing its job. Instead of pulling the fumes out the window, the wind from the outside was pushing the fumes into the classroom. Not good! As the black, sinister looking column nearly reached its peak, students started inhaling the fumes and began coughing.

At first I thought they were being overly dramatic. But the acrid taste of fumes started to settle in the back of my throat. I began coughing. Then I knew they weren't joking and this was serious. Kids were already trying to get out of their chairs and move to the back of the room. There were twenty-five students in the classroom and as they tried to clear free from the fumes, I could see some panic in their eyes. Now kids seemed to be seriously coughing, almost choking; a few were laughing, and all of them were tripping over chairs and trying to escape. I could hear a few kids remark that Mrs. Fillip was trying to kill them. As best I could, I guided them out of the classroom and back into the science lab. The beaker was smoldering at this point. The entire room was filled with the toxic vapors. As they settled back on their lab stools, I could still hear coughing and comments about how they could taste the stuff in their throats. I was a bit unnerved. My heart was pounding. I asked if anyone wanted to go to the nurse. No volunteers. That made me feel a *little* better. In my refrigerator located at the back of the class, I had a 24-pack of bottled water. I quickly distributed one to every student. Everyone in the room seemed to be fine and I started breathing again at a normal pace. The kids started laughing about my unorthodox methods of doing chemistry experiments. Personally, it scared the heck out of me. I had visions of 25 lawsuits being thrust into my faculty mailbox. Once I realized we were all going to live, I told them to stay put while I go back in the classroom to get the beaker. The beaker was still too hot to handle with bare hands. I carried it back to the lab using beaker tongs and placed it on the lab table in the front of the room. Instinctively, some kids moved to the back of the room. I assured them all the vapors had been released and they were safe. The volume of the sucrose and sulfuric acid had increased 300 times the size of the original amount. All that remained was a smoldering piece of black carbon. More oohs and aahs. The kids and I were amazed at this transformation. We started with a clear liquid, combined it with a grainy, white substance, and created a solid, black, mass. I think this qualifies for the "wow" factor. The kids talked about this amazing phenomenon for days. Meanwhile, I continued to be amazed that I didn't asphyxiate my entire classroom.

* * *

October 31. Halloween.

My students had been clamoring for days saying they wanted to do something "cool" on Halloween during science class. I promised them I would come up with something. After searching through some science books, I came up with a nifty idea.

Have you ever heard of goldenrod paper? When you first glance at it, it looks like yellow computer paper. But it is no ordinary paper. Goldenrod paper has been specially treated with a certain type of dye in it. When this treated paper comes in contact with either an acid or a base, the paper acts as an indicator. For example, if you put a cleaning agent on the paper, the ingredients in the cleaning agent, which is a base, react with the dye in the yellow paper and the resulting color is a brilliant shade of red. It looks like blood! Do you already see where I am going with this demonstration? After the paper gets all red, you can put an acid like vinegar on top of the red streaks. Can you guess what happens? The paper turns back to yellow. Aside from any ulterior motive I may have had, the purpose of using this paper was to show the difference between acid and alkaline substances.

When the students came in that morning and settled into class, I explained we were going to continue our class on acids and bases. Groan! "I thought we were going to do something cool today because it's Halloween," one student sourly said. I told them to hang in there. Things might pick up. I pointed out a large jar in the front of the room. It contained a cleaning agent the students used to wipe down their tables after lunch. I didn't say what the liquid was and interestingly, nobody asked what it was either. The only other item on the lab table was a piece of goldenrod paper. I had thrown a few things on top of it to make it look as though I had inadvertently put the paper there. The class began.

"Recently," I told the kids, "scientists have come up with a new way of administering insulin for people who have diabetes. I am lucky to have a friend who works at the diabetes clinic who called me about this new revolutionary idea." I went on to say, "She was more than willing to give me a sample as she is a huge advocate of bringing new ideas into the science classroom. That is what you see in my jar." I explained the liquid was so powerful that people needing insulin merely needed to dip their finger into the solution for 10 seconds ; enough time for the liquid to get in your bloodstream, and from there it goes directly to their pancreas. I could hear the usual ooohs and aaahs. The students were truly amazed at this scientific breakthrough. I continued explaining that if you put more than one finger in the solution, it could become very dangerous. Too much of the liquid on your hand could cause a person to "bleed out." My final point was to explain this special solution also made a superb jewelry cleaner. "Here. Let me demonstrate," I said.

I proceeded to take off my wedding ring and held it over the top of the liquid. "Now watch me as I dip the tip of my ring into the cleaner and see how quickly it shines right up," I said. Of course, this was not *really* the plan! I "accidentally" dropped the ring into the container and it sank right to the bottom. Students were asking, "How are you going to get that out?" I paused, (for effect) and said I would just reach in, grab the ring real fast, and probably nothing would happen to me. The students looked dubious and some even a bit scared. I stuck my hand in the container, fished around for the ring, and then exclaimed, "Oh, my goodness, this stuff is going right into my hand. I can feel it going up my arm. Ow! Ow! It's burning." (Very pained look on my face) After I took my hand out, I turned to Mike who was sitting right next to my table and said, "Mike, quick. Give me a paper towel or something, anything, . . . now." Mike looked around for a second and without thinking, grabbed the nearest thing so I could wipe my hands. Very conveniently, he grabbed the goldenrod paper. "Here, Mrs. Fillip, use this." I grabbed it and began wiping my hands frantically. Instantly the paper turned a bloody red. I could hear gasps. "Oh my gosh, I am bleeding to death," I yelled. I heard gasps, screams, and panic. Two of the students were so alarmed they raced out of the room to get the nurse. I think they must have broken the speed record for the 100-yard dash. More than half the class looked panic-stricken. A student named Andy was sitting on a lab stool right next to the demonstration. When I glanced at him, he was so pale I thought he was going to faint right off the back of the stool.

Two minutes later the nurse rushed into the room with her medical kit after hearing, "Mrs. Fillip is bleeding to death." She was breathless. "What happened? Did you cut yourself?" I didn't think it was a good idea to keep the charade up any longer. A few kids were beginning to notice that once I put the paper down, I had "stopped" bleeding. "No. I'm okay. Just having a little Halloween fun." Sure enough, the truth came out and everyone cracked up laughing. The nurse looked mildly amused but relieved. Andy didn't faint but was glad it wasn't real blood. I was happy to see the color come back into his face. When I saw the nurse later in the day, she suggested I notify her first before doing this kind of experiment. When everything had returned to normal, I told them I had a big surprise for them. I popped open a huge Styrofoam container of dry ice that had been brought in earlier by one of my students' mothers. After explaining the safety rules, I let them play with dry ice. Now that was *"totally cool."*

I REMEMBER WHEN...

I had a parent come in for a conference and she was very upset with me because of the grade I had given her son on a project. I was trying to explain to her the rubric I was using and why her son had failed to meet to the expectations. She was a very nice woman but today she was provoked with me and felt I had graded her son unfairly. I was having a hard time focusing. This woman was a rather large woman and extremely busty. She was wearing a white sweater and I guess it was new. I noticed positioned on her chest was a sticker indicating the size of the sweater, XXL. As she heatedly pointed out that I had done a poor job grading her son, her sweater was bouncing up and down along with the XXL tag. My eyes were drawn to the dancing sticker. Part of me wanted to rip it off. I kept debating whether I should tell her she has a sticker on her sweater or not. Would she be grateful that I had informed her? I mean, it would keep her from further embarrassment the rest of the day. Would she think that I hadn't been paying attention to her tirade about the grade? It was a tough choice. Either way, it definitely kept me from getting upset that she was yelling at me. We worked out the grade issue, and I ended up keeping the sticker a secret. I wondered who the next lucky victim was going to be?

CHAPTER FOURTEEN

Final Stories

"There is no more noble profession than teaching. A great teacher is a great artist, but his medium is not canvas, but the human soul."—Anonymous

My first time ever coaching varsity gymnastics was at a high school with quite a talented team. At the beginning of the season we had several students try out for the team and unfortunately I was not able to carry everyone who tried out. After a few days of tryouts, my team was trimmed down to twelve girls ranging from grades 9-12 all with varying degrees of ability. My philosophy in coaching is this: When I choose girls for a varsity level team they never sit the bench. If they cannot handle the skills needed then I don't put them on varsity. Therefore, everyone participates.

We had a tremendous season, winning just about every competition. When it was time for the state championship, we were seeded number one and the state meet was going to be held in the school where I was coaching. It was a formula for success. As I mentioned before, I believe if you were chosen for the varsity team, then you should have a chance to play or compete. A gymnastic meet consists of vaulting, floor exercise, uneven bars, and balance beam. Four girls per school compete on each event. When a state title is at stake, it would seem reasonable to put your best girls on each piece of equipment. As in the case of many gymnastics teams, there is usually a core of girls who are good at every piece of apparatus. If I had let that core perform on every event, it would have left some girls out of the competition. Many people counseled me that the state meet was the time to put my best girls up. "Don't be a hero and let everyone compete," they told me. "Winning the title is more important."

Prior to the competition, I thought about that statement for a long time. "Winning the title is more important." It just didn't feel right and I wondered how empty these girls would feel if we won the state title and they had not participated. Would they be able to share in the joy of winning? This was high school. Not the Olympics. I made the decision to let every gymnast compete. Every girl on my team was allowed to do their routine on at least one piece of equipment. It was the best decision I ever made. The team spirit was strong and only increased the camaraderie between gymnasts. Everyone supported each other to get ready. They worked tirelessly and were fired up.

The night we had been working toward finally arrived. During the opening ceremony, it was such a heady feeling to walk out onto the mats in *our* school while seeded first. The competition was a fierce battle between all the schools. Gymnasts only get one chance to do their routine in a competition. It's nerve wracking for them. As a coach, you can only hold your breath and hope for the best. The routines you hoped were going to be perfect sometimes were not. The weaker gymnasts often stepped up and performed beautifully. As the competition came to a close, I watched and waited for the scores to come in. The meet was a nail biter. The announcer stepped up to the microphone. We had won the state championship! As my girls lined up to receive their gold medals, I had tears in my eyes because I was so proud of them. All of them! Each and *every* girl made a significant contribution to the first place trophy. They could all walk away knowing that. I walked away never regretting I had allowed twelve girls to become stars that night.

* * *

Put me in front of a crowd and I can talk for days. I have spoken in school, at church, at a conference, and really don't have a problem. I have nerves of steel. Now put me on the piano bench to play Chopin in front of an audience and I am a train wreck. This is rather ironic, as I have never taken a public speaking course. Yet, I have taken years and years of piano lessons, play well, and still my hands become frozen, sweaty, and my belly turns to jelly when I have to perform. I will stumble through a piece I can play perfectly in my own home. I don't get it.

I was teaching at a middle school where it was customary on Memorial Day for the children to go outside and gather around the flagpole. There would be some talks given on the importance of Memorial Day, the pledge of allegiance recited and so forth. At the conclusion of the ceremony two trumpet players would always perform. One player off to the side begins the famous tune, "Taps." Another player, who is hidden in the bushes (that would be me), echoes the same tune with her trumpet. As I mentioned, I cannot seem to relax doing instrumental solos. The band was off on a field trip and they were desperate for a couple of trumpet players. Stupidly, I volunteered knowing how nervous I get. I rationalized this might work because I would be out of sight and no one would know it's me. I practiced out on my deck for a few days and felt confident I could do this. Memorial Day came and we all gathered around the flag pole as I slinked over to the bushes. Just as expected, I was incredibly nervous. Now when you get nervous your respiration rate starts to change. I started talking to myself. "Nancy, calm down. No one can see you. Just relax. You can do this. Breathe slowly. In. Out." It was no use. I was practically hyperventilating. As the first trumpeter sounded out his notes, I blew into my trumpet to respond with the echo. Nothing. No sound came out. No air was coming out of my mouth meaning I was certainly not making any noise. Shoot! The first trumpet player repeated the notes again and waited for me. I took a deep breath and tried again. You could barely hear anything but a few notes sounding like a cat being strangled. No matter how hard I tried to relax and play, I could barely get out a note. The other trumpeter decided to continue on. Without even having a crowd to see me, I was totally unnerved. The other trumpet player finished taps as I sat in the bushes and cried with humiliation. What was wrong with me? I decided to stay in the bushes until the entire school had gone into the building. Peeking out to see if the coast was clear, I ventured back into the building. As I casually walked back into my classroom, I could hear the kids; "Yikes. Did you hear that other trumpet player? What was up with that? Man, they messed up royally. They were awful. Mrs. Fillip, do you know who that was?" I just smiled and said, "I have no clue."

* * *

There was no denying I was one of the teachers in the building, wherever I taught, that liked to give out candy. Partly because I am a candyaholic, there always tended to be a stash lying around in one of my cupboards. Many times when we were playing some educational game or reviewing for a test, candy was a good motivator for kids to pay attention. In fact, I often thought kids would do just about *anything* to get candy in return. Even lick the floor!

We were doing some sort of activity and I had these tiny boxes of Nerds candy to give out. This was a new school for me and I had six classes a day. Remembering all the students' names was a challenge in the first few weeks. We were well into the game and a few students had already won a box of Nerds. When I asked a question, hands shot up in the air. As I scanned the room, I decided to call on this one boy who had been very quiet during the activity. He was holding a box of Nerds. Actually he was holding them for the guy sitting next to him who was bent over tying his shoe. As I looked at this kid, I could not for the life of me remember his name. So I called out to him, "Nerd boy, what do you think?" The class cracked up and I froze for a minute because I didn't see him laughing. Quickly I explained I had only called him that because he was holding the box of Nerds and I could not remember his name. I apologized and said that was very rude of me. He smiled and told me it was fine. I felt relieved. However, the name stuck and he was forever jokingly known as the Nerd boy the entire time he was at that school. He said he didn't mind at all. At the graduation I ran into one of his parents and we struck up a conversation. As we were talking, her son came over and gave me a hug. At the same time, a classmate walked by and said to him, "Congratulations Nerd boy." His mother turned to me and said with a perplexed look on her face, "I have no idea where he ever got that nickname." I quickly turned and looked at her son. He just gave me a wink and wandered off. I looked at his mother and just shrugged.

I REMEMBER WHEN . . .

Robyn had come to the field hockey game and was so proud that she had just had her braces removed at the orthodontist earlier in the afternoon. She was running all over the field smiling and showing everyone her dazzling smile. Back in the 1980's mouth guards were not required for players but highly recommended. I had mentioned to Robyn that her teeth were probably soft after getting her braces off and it would be a good idea to wear her mouth guard for the game. She told me her mother said she *had* to wear a mouth guard.

Robyn was a center forward and a very aggressive player. She had no fear and charged the net with the style of a hungry tiger trying to put the ball in the goal cage. About halfway into the game, the opposing player drove the ball into the goal cage and the goalie kicked it back out without stopping it first. This makes the ball rise up. It flew up right into Robyn's face, right smack into her mouth. Instantly six teeth were sent to the back of her throat. Robyn dropped to the ground screaming. I ran out onto the field and her face was covered with blood. She was choking, gasping, screaming, and spitting out teeth. It was incredibly scary. When Robyn realized I was there she managed to garble out a message to me, "Coach, don't tell my mother I didn't have my mouth guard in." Okay, well, it was a *little obvious* she wasn't wearing her mouth guard. By the way, they were able to get all her teeth back in and she still has her dazzling smile today.

CHAPTER FIFTEEN

Closure

"Goodbye tension, hello pension."—Fay Michaud

A chapter in my life has closed. Because of a recent medical problem, I had to retire from teaching. Recently, I sold all my teaching materials at a garage sale. As strangers pored through and purchased my stuff, I desperately wanted to know what they were going to do with it all. Every gadget and doodad they held up brought back a memory. When they were flipping through my textbooks, I recalled the labs, experiments, and fascinating facts I shared with my classes. I wanted to shout out they couldn't take anything unless they promised to use it to teach somebody. But I just stood there and watched. And I didn't say word. For many months after I retired, I was filled with sadness. Day after day, while I tried to get to the root of the medical problem, I felt unproductive and useless. In addition, I was unable to drive. That seemed like a death sentence. I was dependent on *everyone* to get me *anywhere*. Somehow my mind tricked me into thinking that if I couldn't drive, get to a school to teach, there was no option for me to do anything. Week after week I basked in my misery. I was not fit to live with. My family was patient and understanding of the situation. But I hated what I had become.

This scenario reminded me of the time I had my brain injury. When I came home after being hospitalized for six months, I was angry. Being in a wheelchair and having memory and focus problem was not what I had signed on for at the age of 51. Life was unfair. I didn't know what to do with my anger so I took it out on my family and friends. The house was not tailored to meet the needs of a person in a wheelchair. The doorways were just barely wide enough for me to roll through. All the cabinets above the counters were out of my reach. It was impossible to get close enough to a lamp just to turn it on. During the hot, steamy days of July, (which I hate when I am *not* in a wheelchair), I slammed the wheel chair into doorframes, defied the laws of physics trying to reach for things which often resulted in breakage, and engaged in physical maneuvers which got me hurt. I knew I was making my husband worry but I didn't care.

One month after I came home from the hospital, I woke up one morning and had a heart-to-heart with myself. I knew I was in a bad place. Yes, life was unfair. Isn't that what I tell my students? Ultimately, it came down to choices. I could sit around all day feeling sorry for myself or I could do something about it. Again, this is what I tell my students all the time. "You don't want to fail math? Then you have a choice. You can do nothing or you can start trying." It doesn't mean that you have to do it yourself. I saw the parallels between my students not wanting to ask for help and me not wanting to ask for help. By denying the fact we could not be successful without employing someone's help, we would be stuck in this place forever. I made the decision to start physical therapy, and change my attitude. What a transformation. The doctor told me I might never walk again. I proved him wrong. Just short of a year, I was up and running. Kids who finally overcome their pride and enlist my help as a teacher, gain momentum and dig themselves out of the hole.

This spring, with my medical problem still unresolved, I realized I had been hasty giving away all my teaching supplies. Even though I could not go back to school and teach for another full year, it didn't mean I was done teaching forever. Kind-hearted people tried to give me suggestions of ways I could still teach without being in the classroom. A few months ago I wasn't ready to hear it. But similar to being in a wheelchair, I realized I had choices. Do I sit around all day pouting about no longer having a teaching job or do I become creative and reshape my life? Sometimes I forget I don't have to be defined by my career. Many people are amazed that I would put in years and years of teaching—especially middle school. I loved what I did. I was passionate about where I spent my days. I realized this did not have to stop just because I wasn't in a school. Currently I am a tutor for academics and instrumentals. I *still* teach.

There may have been *moments* in my teaching career where I would have taught differently, or handled a situation in a better way. But there was *never* a moment where I wished I had done something else in my life. Years and years of spending time with youngsters has been exhilarating. A few years ago when I was up at Lake Winnipesaukee in New Hampshire, I was walking on the board walk with my own children. Suddenly I heard, "Hey, Miss Young." That was my maiden name. I whipped around and Marylou came sprinting across the street. She was so excited to see me. Marylou had been a pupil in my class when I was student teaching. "Oh, my gosh, you don't look any different," she exclaimed. I didn't even recognize her. We hugged and I had to ask her name. I had her in class 34 years ago. When she told me her first name, instantly I remembered her last name. She beamed. Excitedly she went on to say she had become a sixth grade teacher because I had inspired her when she was in my class. "When you were my teacher," she said, "I could tell you loved what you were doing. Your enthusiasm was so contagious. When I asked why you wanted to become a teacher, you told me there was no greater calling. You told me kids always want to learn and you wanted to be an inspiration for them. You said that you thought you could make a difference. I never forgot that. That's why I became a teacher." My heart swelled and I could feel the tears start to form in my eyes. I hugged her and told that was the greatest compliment any teacher could ever have. I knew more than ever I had made the right choice 34 years ago.

In closing, the words of William Arthur Ward couldn't sum it up any better:

> "The mediocre teacher tells.
> The good teacher explains.
> The superior teacher demonstrates.
> The great teacher inspires."

WORKS CITED

Askville.com. *http://askville.amazon.com/long-chicken-egg-hatch/ AnswerViewer.do?requestId=8715099 2010.*

Bard IVC Filters "Facts about Mattapoisett, MA." 2009. *http://www.mass. info/mattapoisett.ma/facts.htm.*

Barrett, Erin and Mingo, Jack (2002). "Not Another Apple for the Teacher: Hundreds of Fascinating Facts from the World of Education." New York, New York: Metro Books.

Bellis, Mary. "The History of Xerox." 2010. *http://inventors.about.com/od/ xyzstartinventions/a/xerox.ht*m.

Bloomfield, Louis J. "The Spring Scales Home Page." 1997-2010. www. HowEverythingWorks.org.

Brantley, Amy. "The Greatest Rocker of All Times." 2007. *http://www. associatedcontent.com/article/283780/little_known_facts_about_kiss_legend. html?cat=33*

Canfield, Jack and Hansen, Mark Victor (2002). *Chicken Soup for the Teacher's Soul.* Deerfield Beach, Fl: Health Communications, Inc.

Elkins, David (2003) "Are We Pushing Our Kids Too Hard?" New York, New York: Psychology Today.

Erlbaum, Lawrence "Development of Spatial Cognition." Lawrence Erlbaum Associates. Page 99.

Frank, David V. (2002). *Prentice Hall Science Explorer Chemical Interactions.* Saddle River, New Jersey Page 23.

Frum, David (2000) *How We Got Here: The '70s.* New York, New York: Basic Books. pp. 292-293.

JOC/EFR. "Albert Einstein." April 1997. URL: *www-groups.dcs.st-and. ac.uk/-history/Mathematicians/Einstein.html.*

Newton, Lyn. "Teaching Your Own Child In Your Classroom." 2010. *http:// education.families.com/blog/*teaching-your-own-child-in-your-classroom.

Ohio Central History. "Baby Boomers." July 1, 2005. *http://www. ohiohistorycentral.org/entry.php?rec=1699.*

Ramsey, Robert D. Ed.D (2003). 501 Tips for Teachers. New York, New York: The McGraw-Hill Companies, Inc.

Regan, Patrick (2004). "Teachers: Jokes, Quotes, and Anecdotes." Kansas City, Missouri: Andrews McMeel Publishing, LLC.

Roundtable. "Horace Mann." 2001. *http://www.pbs.org/*kcet/publicschool/innovators/mann.html.

Schulman, Miriam. "Cheating Themselves." Issues in Ethics 1993. *http://www.scu.edu/ethics/publications/iie/v9n1/cheating.html.*

Tomlinson, Carol Ann (2001) *How to Differentiate Instruction in Mixed-Ability Classrooms.* Alexandria, VA: Association for Supervision and Curriculum Development.

Semekovich, Nick "Sodium Still Under Investigation." Sept. 14, 2007. *http://tech.mit.edu/V127/N38/sodiumdrop.html.*

Varnum, Matt. "Smart Use of PowerPoint is Mandatory for Effective Sales." June 23, 2009. *http://blog.presenternet.com/2009/06/23/*smart-use-of-powerpoint-is-mandatory-for-effective-sales/ *http://www.brighthub.com/ office/collabora*tion/articles/13189.aspx.

Whether you're a teacher, a parent, or attended school once in your life, you will be able to laugh and link up with these humorous, poignant, and unforgettable memories of a retired school teacher. Mrs. Fillip talks about what made her decide to become a teacher and the significant changes she experienced over the past thirty-four years. Besides teaching in a public and Catholic school, she had the unique opportunity to teach in an "open classroom" style school as well as a charter school. But the thrust of her book are the tales and anecdotes that involved her students. Mrs. Fillip is an innovative and creative teacher. Never was she afraid to take risks. Exciting labs, experiments, and classroom activities provided stimulating learning visuals the students never forgot. Read how Mrs. Fillip touched many students' lives and how they touched hers.

Edwards Brothers,Inc!
Thorofare, NJ 08086
07 September, 2010
BA2010250